HOW TO FIND YOUR NEW CAREER UPON RETIREMENT

HOW TO FIND YOUR NEW CAREER UPON RETIREMENT

Duane Brown, Ph.D.

Printed on recyclable paper

VGM Career Horizons
a division of *NTC Publishing Group*
Lincolnwood, Illinois USA

Library of Congress Cataloging-in-Publication Data

Brown, Duane.
    How to find your new career upon retirement / Duane Brown.
      p.   cm.
    Includes bibliographical references.
    ISBN 0-8442-4392-2
    1. Job hunting—United States. 2. Retirees—Employment—United
States. I. Title.
HF5382.75.U6B76 1995   94-20725
650.14—dc20   CIP

Published by VGM Career Horizons, a division of NTC Publishing Group
4255 West Touhy Avenue
Lincolnwood (Chicago), Illinois 60646-1975, U.S.A.
© 1995 by NTC Publishing Group. All rights reserved.
No part of this book may be reproduced, stored in a retrieval system,
or transmitted in any form or by any means,
electronic, mechanical, photocopying, recording or otherwise,
without the prior permission of NTC Publishing Group.
Manufactured in the United States of America.

4 5 6 7 8 9 0 ML 9 8 7 6 5 4 3 2 1

Contents

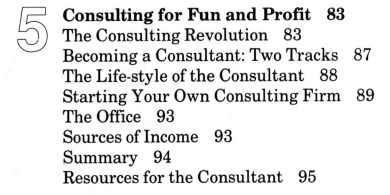

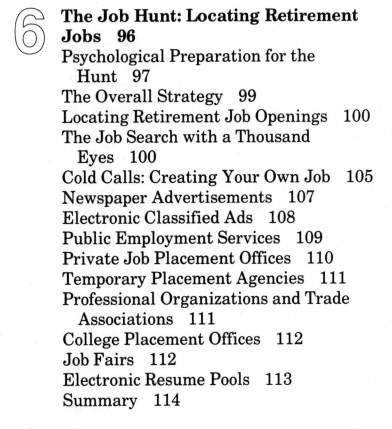

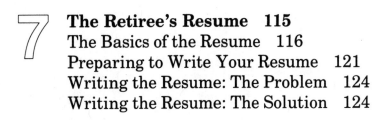

Retirement and Work

1

Did you know that American businesses are facing a growing shortage of younger workers and will have to rely on older workers to remain competitive?

The New Paradox

Retirement! Work? These ideas are incompatible for many people. They dream of moving to places that are warm and sunny, taking control of their time and their lives, and sleeping late. No time clocks to punch. No calls in the middle of the night. No overtime. No fighting the crowds on weekends for tee times. No ties, boring business lunches, deadlines, meetings to attend, planes to catch, or quotas to meet. No job! It is a dream realized by many people.

Some workers' dreams of a carefree retirement are being interrupted by the nightmare of reality. Their non-working "future" is being thrust upon them by what is variously called restructuring, downsizing, or reduction in force. Retirement is coming like an early frost, nipping plans for the future in the bud and forcing a reconceptualization of the present. A "retired" IBM employee summed up his experience as follows: "I'll have a good income, but it won't be enough to meet my family's needs. And I can't imagine myself playing golf for the next 25 years. I have to find a new career."

Others who retired at a time and under the conditions of their choosing have discovered a considerable discrepancy between the reality of retirement and the Shangri-la they envisioned. Many of these people didn't understand how vital their career was to their emotional well-being. One retiree said, "I never learned to play. I now know that I didn't because my self-image was tied entirely to being a worker. When I retired, my self-image went to hell because I wasn't working. A year of therapy has helped, but not as much as getting another job." One in three retirees returns to some form of work within a year of leaving his or her job. Others go directly from their jobs to new careers. The reasons for their actions are as varied as the workers themselves.

I'm Bored

Some retirees, even some who didn't like their jobs, did not realize how their work literally established the agenda for their lives until they retired. Their jobs dictated when they got up in the morning and how they filled many of their waking hours and even provided a leisure agenda in the form of after-work stopovers at local bars, office parties, and company picnics. As one worker put it, "When I wasn't working, I was thinking about working, planning for work, or talking to one of my co-workers about working." Some people who are engrossed in their work are overwhelmed by the amount of free time they have available after retirement, and boredom is often the result. One retiree would visit her old business every day just to see "how things were going."

Often workers cannot anticipate their lives when every day is a holiday. Retirement simply does not offer the challenges of the working world, and some retirees sorely miss those challenges. For these people, a gnawing and persistent feeling of not having enough to do begins after six to ten months of retirement. Soon the boredom builds to an overpowering drive to find something to do. At this point, a retirement career is only as far away as the time it takes to locate it.

Where does my money go? And then there are those workers who simply underestimated their financial needs after retirement and found that they either had to curtail their life-style or go back to work. Retirement planners provide various guidelines for estimating financial needs after retirement, and most typically they determine that retirees will need 80 percent as much money during retirement as they did during their working years to maintain their life-styles. However, these estimates are for groups and not for individuals and are predicated on the idea that the mortgage will be paid off, children will be self-supporting, and there will be no catastrophic health problems that require unusual medical expenses. Many retirees, particularly those forced into early retirement, do not meet these guidelines.

However, a more pervasive problem has resulted in lower-than-expected retirement incomes for many people: the change in interest rates. Retirees are quite understandably interested in capital preservation and, as a result, invest their nest eggs in insured savings accounts and government bonds and notes, in spite of warnings to the contrary by financial experts. A decade ago, retirees could count on earning 8 to 12 percent or more on their investments, and many retirees expected these yields to continue. Today these same people are earning 3 to 6 percent on their investments, and their life-styles are suffering.

Then there are those people who made "safe" investments only to see them turn sour. Some retirees invested in IBM, that paragon of American business, only to see their net worth plummet by 50 percent and their dividend cut by 55 percent. Unfortunately, there is much financial uncertainty on the horizon for present and future retirees. Taxes on Social Security, reduction of Medicare benefits, underfunded pension plans, and an uncertain economic future for the United States erode income and confidence. One result: many retirees find themselves with inadequate financial resources to maintain their life-style and, in some instances, to provide adequate food, shelter, and other necessities. Another result is the fear that these circumstances may arise. Less income, or the fear that financial resources will be inadequate, are causing people to enter retirement careers.

I want to give something back

There is a large group of people who retire and no longer want to hold a job in the traditional sense but wish to make a contribution to others and add meaning to their lives. As one retiree put it, "I've done well, and I just want to give something back at this point. Being a volunteer allows me to make a contribution, but it also allows me to control my life. Also, I don't feel guilty when I tell the volunteer coordinator that I'm going to be gone for the month of January and she needs to find a replacement. I could never have done that when I was working." Some people might take issue with the idea that volunteering is work, because they equate getting paid and working. However, it is likely that those people have never volunteered. One need go no further than local hospitals or schools to see not only how hard volunteers work but what an impact they can make.

Retirees work for many reasons. Forty-five percent of all workers are either still in the labor force if they are over 65, or, if they are younger, expect to be holding down a job after 65, according to a *U.S. News* survey.

It's my turn

Many housewives feel trapped when their husbands retire and they are left with the same old chores. Some are deciding that it is their turn to explore new roles and are entering retirement careers. Not surprisingly, in many cases, both men and women have felt trapped in their careers because of the need to provide economic security for their families. With children leaving home and an income from a pension plan or Social Security, the trap is sprung, and they feel free to pursue unforgotten dreams. They feel their retirement presents them with their last opportunity to take risks, to tap potential that has long been ignored, or simply to turn one of their hobbies into the enjoyable career that they have wanted but were unable to attain. Often this pent-up need to tap an unrealized ambition blossoms into glorious bloom in a retirement career. One professional golfer on the Seniors circuit, Walter Zembriski, was employed as a steel worker until his children were educated and he could take the risk of leaving the security of his job. At age 50, he joined the Seniors professional golf tour, and in 1993, his earnings far exceeded those of a steel worker.

Some terms

Before we proceed further, it is important that I define some of the concepts that I will be using, since they depart to some degree from standard usage. When workers leave their jobs or are forced to do so, they enter a period of time in their lives called *retirement*. Workers, whether they retire voluntarily or involuntarily, typically receive some form of *retirement income*, which may or may not be sufficient to meet their needs. *Life-style* is used to denote the totality of a retiree's existence, including work, leisure, and other planned and unplanned activities. A *retirement job* is a paid or unpaid job that a worker enters after he or she has begun retirement. A person holding an unpaid job is a *volunteer*. *Leisure* is unpaid use of discretionary time that does not involve the production of goods or services. Workers often pursue leisure as an outlet for the tension that results from holding a job. A *retirement career* is all the paid and unpaid jobs a retiree holds after he or she re-enters the work force.

Do You Know Where You Are Going?

The importance of planning your retirement cannot be overstated, but Americans are often not good planners. A Gallup survey that I codirected revealed that about 60 percent of American workers are in jobs because of chance, the influence of family and friends, or job availability. Only 40 percent developed a plan to get into their careers. It is no wonder that 65 percent of adults would try to get more information about jobs if they could start over. Lots of people spend years stuck in jobs they don't like, and the last thing they want is to be stuck in a retirement life-style that is unappealing. Getting stuck can only be avoided by careful planning and then making informed decisions.

Sure I have a plan—it's around here somewhere

Why don't people plan? Some people are pessimists. They do not believe they can influence their own destiny. For them, life is one big roller coaster ride with sudden ups and downs, turns and thrills. For these people, the future is unknowable and uncontrollable. Some naive optimists don't plan either. For them, life is a beach with endless sunshine and good times. They believe that the future will take care of itself. Odd as it sounds, some people do not plan because they are afraid they will fail. They would rather take their chances with fate than risk making the wrong plan. Are you a pessimist or a naive optimist? Are you fearful that your planning efforts may not bear the fruit that you hope for? If so, it is time to recognize the importance of planning. Dozens of studies suggest that carefully setting goals and then developing plans to achieve those goals is not only worthwhile but necessary for success. Indicate your own stance on the future by writing a *yes* before each of the following statements if you agree or a *no* if you disagree. Planners put a *yes* before most of these statements.

_____ I am a goal setter.

_____ I am in control of my own destiny.

_____ I have a financial game plan for retirement.

_____ I believe that there is more than one path to success, and I regularly develop a second plan—plan B.

_____ If life is a crapshoot, I know ways to load the dice.

_____ I always have a scheme to make things go my way.

Some people don't plan because they simply don't have the information they need. If you ask most Americans where the jobs will be in the future, they will invariably say in computers and medicine, but when asked to elaborate, they are hard-pressed to give details. Because of the publicity focused on the shortage of nurses, many people are now aware that there are large numbers of openings in this field. But most people are unaware that the publicity about nurses is likely to result in a vast oversupply of registered nurses before the end of this decade. Even fewer people know that there are large numbers of jobs available for nurse's assistants, positions that require as little as three months of training. Similarly, many people are unaware that we face a shortage of younger workers in this country.

I'll plan for tomorrow—tomorrow

Your approach to planning your life after retirement and the urgency for you to plan will be dependent upon many factors, not the least of which is the circumstances under which your retirement began. If you were forced into early retirement, you may feel that you are simply too young to retire. If you made your own decision to retire, you may take another approach.

Recently I spoke to a 62-year-old who was going to retire two weeks after our conversation. When I asked him about his retirement plan, he indicated that he was going to "play it by ear," and if he didn't like retirement without a job, he would "find something to do." As our conversation continued, it was clear that he not only had chosen the time to leave his current job, but he had saved a substantial amount of money in preparation for his retirement. The amount of money that you have at the time of retirement will influence your approach to planning and may influence not only whether you seek a retirement career but the type of career you enter as well.

Financial security and the nature of your retirement (voluntary or involuntary) are not the only factors that will influence your life-style planning process. Your personal view of yourself as a retired person will also influence how you approach this vital transition. One airlines captain bought a ranch in west Texas five years prior to retirement. When asked why he was going into ranching he replied, "I never want to be introduced as a former airlines captain." Clearly the meaning this captain attached to retirement was that it was the end of a chapter in his life, and he could take control of his life by beginning another career.

Some retirees do not have this pilot's foresight. They view retirement as a wonderful new life where they are freed from the shackles of paid employment, only to learn that they have traded one set of problems for another. They begin their retirement career and then realize that something is missing from their lives: a job. Unlike the captain who planned ahead, these people are unable to accurately predict their own retirement behavior. In some instances, they simply deny the obvious: their personal sense of well-being is tied to being productive.

Whether the process of choosing a retirement career begins five years prior to or three years after retirement, it is an important decision that varies to some degree from other career choices. However, like most decision-making processes, it is likely to result in a more satisfactory outcome if it is begun prior to retirement and if some simple rules are followed. One of these rules is to fully understand how your own motivation relates to career choice. As human beings, we are motivated by two sets of factors: rewards and punishments. When we leave our jobs, we are often fleeing from situations that we view as negative or punishing. This perception is coupled with the expectation that what lies ahead—retirement—will be more rewarding or satisfying. In order for our expectations to be realized, the retirement years must be filled with experiences that are meaningful. For many this will mean holding down a part- or full-time retirement job, even though it is dissimilar to the one that they left.

A successful outcome is also dependent upon understanding the retirement careers open to you. It is very clear that most Americans are largely unaware of the 12,000 jobs in our labor force and how they might gain access to those jobs.

Finally, your choice of a retirement career must be made in the context of your other life roles, which for many include spouse, parent, grandparent, leisurite, and community member. A recent issue of *Business Week* featured an 81-year-old worker who had just reduced his workweek from 55 to 49 hours. He had embarked upon a retirement career after six months of retirement and had obviously made his new career the centerpiece of his "retirement." Most retirees want more out of life than work, even when they continue their employment.

I'd plan if I knew what to consider

The mechanics of choosing a retirement career are in some senses different from those involved in making an initial career choice or a midlife career choice. Why? Because in many cases, not working is an option. So is part-time employment. Volunteering is also an option that most workers could not consider when they were making initial or transitional career choices because they needed to earn money to support themselves and their families. Another variable that sometimes enters the picture is that retirees can choose the option of continuing in their current position with a reduced workload or assume another position. It has long been common practice for physicians, dentists, lawyers, and other professionals to phase themselves out of their practices over time. Some retirees in other types of jobs have this option as well.

Criteria used by workers at different life stages to choose careers may vary. Younger workers may be more concerned about opportunities for advancement and salary increases, while older workers may focus on the extent to which the career accommodates their retirement life-style, but the criteria for making these choices may also vary more by individual than by age group.

How To Limit Myself Without Even Trying

While there are important differences between choosing initial and midlife careers and retirement careers, there are some important similarities as well. One important similarity is that decision making must overcome what I term *self-limiting stereotypes*. People with self-limiting stereotypes have beliefs about themselves that are mostly untrue, but they act as if these beliefs are true. Because retirees are older, many of their self-limiting stereotypes are related to age. Check your self-limiting stereotypes by completing the following quiz.

TRUE OR FALSE

1. _____ It is common for retirees to die soon after giving up their jobs because they feel worthless.

2. _____ It is more difficult for people over 60 to learn because of diminished memory and mental capacity, and, thus, retraining is less of a possibility.

3. _____ Older workers miss more work because of failing health.

4. _____ Older workers have lower productivity than their younger counterparts because of their physical condition.

5. _____ Older workers are faced with greatly reduced job opportunities because of age discrimination.

6. _____ A person who is 60 is old.

Four of the five questions posed above are false, and one, number 5, is at least partially false. A few retirees die soon after retirement, but that is coincidental: they would have died if they had continued to work. There can be no doubt that being happy leads to a longer life or that a person who becomes acutely depressed because of leaving work might die sooner because of the stress resulting from the depression. However, retirees typically do not die because they are unhappy in retirement. One of the questions, number 6, is true only if you believe it to be so. The average 60-year-old male has a life expectancy of 17 years, and the average women can expect to live nearly a quarter of a century at 60, so the perception that a person is old at 60 is in conflict with all biological data. Perhaps their longer life expectancy explains why women are slightly more likely than men to pursue retirement careers.

Many older people see themselves as having a diminished ability to learn. Research shows that while the ability to memorize material may be slightly reduced in older people, they have developed coping mechanisms that allow them to learn as well as younger workers. The biggest barrier to learning for older workers is lack of self-confidence growing out of this self-limiting stereotype, and it is highly likely that they will have to learn something new to get a retirement career. Sixty percent of retired workers seeking new jobs had to acquire new knowledge or skills, according to an AARP survey in *Modern Maturity*, 1989. The good news is that this extra education paid off. Although more than 60 percent of retired workers were working less and earning less, more than 30 percent were earning more. Those who started their own businesses were earning the most. Perhaps more to the point, they were engaged successfully in retirement careers.

Older workers are more reliable and just as productive as their younger counterparts. Moreover, as many companies know, older workers are more loyal than younger workers. The AARP survey also found that older workers stayed with their companies five times longer than workers who were younger. The irony here is that some companies have attempted to energize their operations by infusing younger workers into them.

We know that age discrimination exists, but we are unsure of the extent to which it limits older workers. Federal law prohibits discrimination against older workers, defined as anyone over 40, and recent court cases have resulted in substantial penalties for businesses that have engaged in age discrimination. Conversely, some businesses are openly courting retirees because of their reliability, work ethic, and loyalty. For example, American Airlines has made an effort to hire older workers and in November of 1992 graduated a 55-year-old flight attendant from its training program in Dallas. What's more, she wasn't the oldest graduate of their programs. Other companies such as McDonald's and some hotel chains have made similar efforts with varying results.

Another important similarity between choosing a retirement career and a career at other life stages is that the entire life-style must be considered. Younger workers may not be as concerned about opportunities for leisure as are older workers, but they are concerned about the community in which they live, working conditions and opportunities for spouses.

Subsequent chapters will explore the types of occupations that may be most attractive to retirees. The remainder of this chapter will be devoted to helping engage in some self-exploration so that you can begin to answer ques-

tions relating to your needs and values and how these relate to a satisfactory retirement career and life-style.

Do I Have To Look Ahead?
You will have a future. It is up to you whether you will
plan it. Social scientists have long understood that planning is of major importance when predicting personal success and satisfaction. If you do decide to plan, you can get
some clues about directions to take by examining your current life space. Begin by estimating how much time you
spend per week in each of the following areas. If you are retired, base your estimates on your life when you were
working. Keep in mind that, theoretically at least, each of
us has approximately 112 waking hours per week available to us.

TYPICAL WEEK

1. _____ How many hours per week do you spend preparing for work or working? This includes
volunteer activities, such as union commit-
tees, and any secondary jobs you may have.
Also include commuting to and from work in
this category.

2. _____ How many hours per week do you spend in
leisure activities? This includes activities
such as watching television, reading, visiting with friends, engaging in sports such as
golf or tennis.

3. _____ How many hours do you spend in family-
related activities?

4. _____ How many hours per week do you spend in
religious activities?

5. _____ How many hours per week do you spend in
volunteer (unpaid) activities not related to
your work?

6. _____ How many hours per week do you spend in
household activities, including cleaning,
cooking, repair work, washing, budgeting,
personal care, lawn care, shopping, auto
care?

_____ Total hours spent

Now, if you could have an ideal week doing entirely as you wished, how would you allocate your time?

_____ 1. Work

_____ 2. Leisure activities

_____ 3. Family activities

_____ 4. Religious activities

_____ 5. Volunteer activities

_____ 6. Household activities

_____ Total hours spent

Your first list represents the reality of your life as a worker, particularly the reality that paid employment takes up a large block of time. When you stepped into your fantasy and began to imagine your ideal schedule, your values came to the fore. The second list most likely reflects the value you place on the various roles in your life at this time. If the allocation of time in the second list approximates that in the first list, you may be saying, "Is what I'm doing now really what I value?" It may also suggest that you will have some difficulty giving up your job and may need to seek paid employment after retirement. If you are currently retired, do you prefer the schedule you had when you were working? If you answer "yes," it is probably time to get on with choosing a retirement career.

What Is It I Really Believe?

Another way of looking at ourselves and how we will function in the future is to examine our values. Our values are the most fundamental part of our belief system and, as such, usually guide our behavior. They also influence how we think and shape our emotions regarding people and things. For example, whether we support conservative or liberal politicians depends upon the degree to which their political stance reflects our own values. When we find ourselves agreeing or disagreeing with a person or group, liking or disliking, approaching or avoiding a person or situation, our values are involved.

Values do guide our behavior, but there are times when we act in ways that are incompatible with our values, and, when we do, the result is that we are at best unhappy and at worst depressed. Sometimes people are forced by circumstances to violate their own beliefs. For example, a hungry person who is essentially honest steals to keep from starving. That person may feel guilty, even though he or she had to steal to survive. Similarly, retirees may become depressed even though they had very little choice in the matter. However, a person who chooses to retire may feel just as bad even though he or she had complete control of the decision if that decision violates his or her basic values. One of the major reasons that people are unhappy in their jobs is because those jobs do not satisfy their values. Similarly, one of the reasons that retirees are unhappy is that their retirement life-style is at odds with their basic beliefs, their values.

As odd as it seems, one of the most frequent reasons that people violate their own values is because they do not plan carefully, and circumstances result that are incompatible with their fundamental beliefs. It is a well-known fact that large numbers of workers in this country are unhappy with their careers. Why? Because only 40 percent of them developed a conscious plan to enter a career and pursued it. The rest were influenced by others, took the only job available, or got their job by luck or chance circumstances. My guess is that fewer than 40 percent think carefully about the importance of work at the time they are considering their retirement options. Probably fewer still fail to consider the importance of their overall life-style.

Values associated with satisfaction on the job and elsewhere can be classified into many categories. For example, some people value money and status, and unless they have both, they will not be satisfied. If their job is the only way that this value is satisfied and they leave it, dissatisfaction will be the result. Other people value artistic endeavor, and unless they are being creative or supporting creative work in a leisure activity, they feel unfulfilled. Still others value association with their peers, and to take away that support without fully considering the impact of that decision can lead to unhappiness. The point here is simple: our values need to be satisfied. If we ignore them at the time of retirement, the last 20 or more years of our lives may be unhappy ones.

It is easy to predict that if you choose a retirement career that is incompatible with your values, you will be unhappy. Moreover, if that job is incompatible with the type of retirement life-style you seek, you will be unhappy. If you value the acquisition of wealth, you may be unable to stop working because of the loss of income. Having strong spiritual values may lead you to a number of careers, but they may also lead you into a variety of volunteer jobs. People who are altruistic often try to help others, but they may also enjoy volunteer activities that are related to helping people, saving the environment, or fostering more humane treatment of animals. Conversely, selecting a retirement life-style that does not allow the altruistic to satisfy their values by engaging in altruistic activities would be a major mistake.

Why Choose A Retirement Career?

It's obvious. To make money, to improve your self-esteem, to stay out of your spouse's way, for companionship, because you are a lousy golfer or bridge player, because you hate daytime television. Each person has his or her own reasons for continuing to work. The remainder of this book is designed to help you discover your own reasons.

Summary: Successful Transition Or Rough Crossing?

Your transition to a satisfactory retirement life-style and beyond will depend upon a number of factors. Planning to avoid trivialization may be chief among these. If your job has ended or will end soon, you must go about reconstructing the meaning of your life. If working is important to you, this probably means that a retirement career is in your future. If you fail to plan, you may be lucky, and your retirement years may be fulfilling, but you are taking a big chance with the rest of your life, and your luck may not hold.

As a retiree, you have literally dozens of decisions to make. Should I seek paid employment? Unpaid employment? If "yes," where should I look? Will anyone hire an older worker, and, if so, what types of problems will I face? It has been years since I looked for a job. What job-hunting skills do I need, particularly as an older worker? What type of life-style should I try to establish, and how does my career fit into my overall retirement plan? These and other questions will be addressed in the pages to come.

Choosing a Retirement Life-style

Did you know that one-half of all people who retire return to some type of work within a year after retirement?

To Career or Not Career   Will Shakespeare will have to forgive me, but the question is whether you should enter a retirement career. The answer to this question may also actually answer the more fundamental question of "To be or not to be" posed by Hamlet. While this Shakespearean metaphor can be carried only so far, no retirees want to weather the slings and arrows that retirement can bring. They want to be satisfied with the life they choose and not be bored, depressed, or both. While there are few guarantees, one truism is that you can dramatically increase the probability of a satisfactory retirement by careful planning.

Use Your Imagination

Take a few minutes at this time to imagine the type of retirement life-style that will be best for you and your personality. In this process, try to avoid the "shoulds" and "oughts" of others. Friends and associates may say, "You're retiring; you should begin to think about relocating." Or, "You shouldn't take their offer of part-time employment. It's not fair to you." And still others will say, "You should stop working and enjoy yourself. You've earned it." Other people can give you useful advice, but you are the only one who can successfully construct a plan for the remainder of your life. As you try to get a clear image of what would be the best retirement life-style for you, consider the following options.

• Work–Work–Work: In this option, you either stay in your current occupation or choose another full-time job. Other life roles such as leisure activities participant, family member, and citizen will remain as they are. Think about your life one year, five years, and ten years from this point in time. Imagine yourself living as you do now.

• Work–Play–Other: In this option, you continue to work, but on a part-time basis. In this scenario, you have the freedom to expand other life roles such as leisure activities participant, family member, and citizen. You also have an income to supplement your retirement income. However, you will still be tied to a work schedule, and your other life roles will be curtailed accordingly. Again, imagine yourself at various times in your future as you work part-time and expand your other life roles. As you work less, what roles would be expanded to occupy the free time that results? This is the most common scenario for retirees who decide to work. Would it be satisfying for you?

• Work (no pay)–Play–Other: In this scenario of the future, you replace work with volunteering. Volunteering provides you with a vast array of work opportunities but allows you the flexibility to expand your other life roles. Volunteering also allows you to give something back to society, because many opportunities to volunteer entail helping the ill or disenfranchised poor, making contributions to causes such as cleaning up the environment, enhancing the education of children or adults, or improving the political process by registering voters or campaigning for candidates who will make a difference. Try to imagine yourself in this life-style. How would you feel about working for no pay? Jimmy Carter is probably the best-known person who lives this lifestyle. You are not a past president of the United States, but you may be involved in something that is very meaningful to you. If you leave it, how will you react?

• Play–Play–Other: This is the option that many preretirees dream about. It gives you complete control of your time. It also presents you with the task of generating meaningful options. You can spend as much or as little time as you want in leisure, visit the grandchildren whenever you wish, sleep late. One retired couple sleeps late, watches the morning news shows, plays a round of golf, takes a nap, plays cards or reads, and visits friends or goes out to dinner when they are not traveling or visiting relatives. They must, of course, handle the routine chores of living, such as shopping, cooking, and maintaining their house and car, but they spend no time in either unpaid or paid work. Think about how you would respond if you were placed in this life-style. Would you be satisfied? Bored?

For Married Couples Only

As you consider what retirement life-style to choose, it is important to consider first what each marital partner requires for satisfaction as a retiree. Some women assume that they should retire when their husbands do, only to find that they are retiring to the unstimulating role of a homemaker, a role they wanted to abandon when they went to work. Some men avoid retirement because of what Chapman, in his book *Comfort Zones,* refers to as the "honey-do" effect: they are afraid that if they retire their wives will say "honey do" this and "honey do that." It is also likely that marital problems that may have been conveniently ignored in the hustle and bustle of your working lives may emerge as fullblown crises in retirement. If you want to stay married, identify what each of you require in a retirement life-style and then, through negotiation, adopt a couples life-style. Remember, you are not joined at the hip, and if the plan that you adopt is not mutually satisfying, the result may be that you trade the stress of pre-retirement for a different set of problems that is equally as problematic.

Decisions, Decisions: How to Choose

How can you decide which of the life-styles described above is best suited for you? First, what is your emotional response as you imagine yourself in each scenario? If you get a feeling ranging from queasy-uneasy to out-and-out discomfort, proceed with caution. However, those feelings may simply be the result of not thinking carefully about your retirement future. In this section, I want to suggest that you consider certain critical factors prior to leaping into what may be an unsuitable choice.

How much money will I need?

A current television advertisement suggests that there is nothing as catastrophic as outliving your money. Most people would agree, and thus planning a retirement life-style necessarily begins by considering the amount of money you will have available to you under varying circumstances. If you decide that you will not have the money you need, then the need to select a retirement career is heightened.

How much will I need? Earlier I suggested that the typical recommendation is that you will need 80 percent as much money during your retirement years as you do prior to retirement. However, a basic financial principal is that you will need to plan your retirement so that your income increases 3 to 5 percent per year on average to account for inflation. The implications of this latter statement are staggering. If it takes $20,000 to fund your retirement life-style in 1994, it will take $44,000 to fund an equivalent life-style in 2014 if the rate of inflation averages 4 percent over the 20 intervening years. Let me give you a personal example. Ten years ago, I started drawing a small annuity of $3,650 per year. Since that time, my annuity has decreased to $3100, a decrease of 15 percent. During that same period, the cost of living has increased by nearly 35 percent. Obviously two factors were at work: my income was going down, and my costs were going up. Had I been relying on the annuity as the sole source of my retirement income, my spending would have had to be reduced by 50 percent. Many retirees will find themselves in the same situation unless they plan wisely.

The best place to start planning for the future is to determine your current expenses and contrast these with retirement expenses. Think about the amount of money you spend per month, and then try to project what your expenses would be if you maintained your current life-style. Undoubtedly some of your current expenses will go down, but others may go up. For example, if you plan to stay in your home, maintenance and property taxes will probably go up, and mortgage payments may drop to nil. You may also decide to eliminate your savings plan at the time of retirement. To get an estimate of your expenses, complete the worksheet on the following two pages.

Monthly Expenses

HOUSING		CURRENT	RETIREMENT
Rent or mortgage payment (Do not include property taxes here)		_____	_____
Maintenance (include condominium fees)		_____	_____
Utilities/services		_____	_____
Gas		_____	_____
Electricity		_____	_____
Water		_____	_____
Cable TV		_____	_____
Telephone		_____	_____
Household upkeep (e.g., furniture, linens)		_____	_____
TOTAL HOUSING	A.	$_____	_____

TRANSPORTATION COSTS			
Car payments (including leases)		_____	_____
Fuel		_____	_____
Maintenance (including repairs and routine service for gas and oil)		_____	_____
Licenses and registration		_____	_____
Parking		_____	_____
Bus fare/taxi/mass transportation		_____	_____
TOTAL TRANSPORTATION	B.	$_____	_____

FOOD			
Groceries		_____	_____
Dining out		_____	_____
TOTAL FOOD	C.	$_____	_____

CLOTHING			
Purchases		_____	_____
Laundry/dry cleaning/repair		_____	_____
TOTAL CLOTHING	D.	$_____	_____

MEDICAL (EXCEPT INSURANCE)		**CURRENT**	**RETIREMENT**
Doctor/dentist		_____	_____
Medicine		_____	_____
TOTAL MEDICAL	E.	$_____	_____
INSURANCE/SAVINGS			
Automobile		_____	_____
Health (including Medicare supplement)		_____	_____
Household		_____	_____
Liability		_____	_____
Life/disability		_____	_____
Savings		_____	_____
TOTAL INSURANCE/SAVINGS	F.	$_____	_____
PERSONAL			
Cosmetologist/barber		_____	_____
Health spa		_____	_____
Cosmetics		_____	_____
Gifts		_____	_____
Donations		_____	_____
Child care		_____	_____
Pet care		_____	_____
Lessons/other		_____	_____
TOTAL PERSONAL	G.	$_____	_____
RECREATION			
Travel		_____	_____
Memberships/fees		_____	_____
Magazines/newspapers		_____	_____
Entertainment		_____	_____
TOTAL RECREATION	H.	$_____	_____
TOTAL ALL EXPENSES	(A-H)	$_____	_____

Now that you have estimated your retirement expenses, you need to make an accurate estimate of your retirement income. Again, start with your current income and then project what your income will be at the time of retirement.

Monthly Income

SOURCES	CURRENT	RETIREMENT
Salaries and wages	_____	_____
Pension plan/annuities	_____	_____
Social Security payments	_____	_____
Interest on deposits	_____	_____
Royalties	_____	_____
Income from investments	_____	_____
Rental income	_____	_____
Other (such as alimony)	_____	_____
TOTAL GROSS INCOME	$_____	_____
TAXES ON INCOME		
Federal income tax	_____	_____
State income tax	_____	_____
Local taxes (including property taxes)	_____	_____
Intangibles tax	_____	_____
TOTAL TAXES	$_____	$_____

CURRENT GROSS INCOME – TAXES = NET INCOME $_____

RETIREMENT GROSS INCOME – TAXES = NET INCOME $_____

NET RETIREMENT INCOME – NET RETIREMENT EXPENSES = $_____

If your projected income is greater than your projected expenses, you should be able to maintain your life-style at the time of retirement. If it is less, you may be able to increase your savings and investments and enhance your income at the time of retirement. You may also wish to diminish your life-style at the time you quit working.

As mentioned at the beginning of this section, the unknowns in the financial equation are inflation and, in some instances, income. If it takes $40,000 to finance your retirement life-style in the year 2000, it will increase to $49,000 by the year 2005 if the inflation rate is 4 percent; $53,600 if the inflation rate is 6 percent; and a whopping $64,400 if the annual rate of inflation is 10 percent, according to Sylvia Porter's *Your Finances in the 1990s.* In some instances, your retirement income will be under your control. However, the inflation rate will not be subject to your control. Neither will the stock and bond market or interest rates paid on savings. At best, your retirement income will be somewhat variable.

Before you proceed, you need to make a preliminary decision about your need for additional income at the time of retirement from your current job. For some, that will be very easy to estimate. For others, the decision will be more difficult. If there is any doubt about your ability to fund your retirement life-style, start considering a retirement career. If your income will support the retirement life-style you desire, other variables need to be considered before making a final decision about your life-style.

How Good Is My Health?

At age 60, the average male has a life expectancy of 17 years, and the average female can expect to live an additional 21 years. While some people pronounce themselves old at this age, the facts are that the 60-year-old who is in good health and physical condition can maintain the pace of much younger people. The typical 60-year-old has plenty of time to enter and succeed in a new career. However, when an individual is deciding whether to work, averages are of little benefit. Men and women must consider the status of their own health in making this decision, and, if health is a problem, their life-style options may be severely restricted. Employers want healthy workers for a variety of reasons, including health insurance costs and the specter of reduced productivity because of employee illness. In the "leaner and meaner" workplace of today, higher productivity is not just an expectation, it is a mandate for business survival.

If your health is poor, you should consider a life-style option that will enable you to care for yourself most effectively. If you are healthy but appear unhealthy because of obesity or simply being out of shape, these factors need to be corrected to maximize your opportunities in the workplace. If you have bad habits, such as smoking or drinking too much, you need to change them to increase your ability to compete. If you are healthy, look it, and have the eating, drinking, nonsmoking, and exercise habits to maintain your health, your options are wide open.

Relocate for Life-style?   Every geographic location offers differing life-style options. Some provide myriads of leisure options while offering few occupational opportunities. In these situations, a person can greatly expand his or her leisure role. In other locales, the reverse is true, and thus continuing to work can be a viable option. Some people, because they currently live in proximity to their relatives, can easily increase their involvement in the family role. You need to begin by considering the options offered by your current location. Begin this process by answering the following questions.

Evaluating My Current Location

_____ 1. Can I stay in my current job, or are other jobs readily available if I decide to work?

_____ 2. Are there types of volunteer activities available that I would enjoy?

_____ 3. Are the leisure activities I enjoy readily available when I want to participate in them?

_____ 4. Is the proximity of my family suitable to me at this time?

_____ 5. Can I get involved in community, church, and other activities that will be of interest to me in retirement?

_____ 6. Is the climate in my current location suitable?

_____ 7. Can I improve my financial situation by moving to another location where the cost of living is lower (e.g., housing, income taxes, property taxes, inheritance taxes, sales taxes, health care, services)?

The answer to these questions may be critical in choosing a life-style and deciding whether to relocate. However, to fully explore this issue, you must also consider the positives and negatives of moving. Because we are a mobile society, we also have the option of changing the nature of our opportunities by relocating, and that is precisely what thousands of retirees do each year. Orlando, Florida, provides the greatest opportunities for retirees who wish to work, according to David Savageau's book *Retirement Places Rated.* The Fort Meyers, Florida, area gets the highest rating in terms of providing leisure opportunities, according to this same source. However, what Savageau overlooks are the psychological factors that must be considered when relocating. One of these is the stress of moving. Another has to do with the loss of contact with loved ones and friends and the diminishment of the family role. In order to determine whether you are willing to move to accommodate a life-style change, please answer the following questions "yes" or "no."

Relocation and Change in Psychological Stressors

_____ 1. A move to a new location would hamper my ability to deal with family matters, such as assisting aging parents.

_____ 2. A move would result in the loss of valued associates and friends.

_____ 3. I would have difficulty making new friends because of the kind of person I am.

_____ 4. There are places and events associated with my current residence that I would miss.

_____ 5. A move to the new area I am considering would increase my financial need because of the increased cost of living, taxes, trips to see friends and relatives.

If you answered "yes" to questions 1-5, then a move will decrease the social support in your life at a time when people need it most. If you answered "yes" to question 5, a move from your current location may increase your stress level at a time when your goal is probably to reduce it. This does not mean that other considerations, such as the ability to pursue a retirement career or to engage in leisure activities on a year-round basis, may not be more important. It does mean that you may need to consider your options carefully, perhaps to the point of making a trial move to the "desired" location before burning your bridges. In the final analysis, the geographic area you choose should accommodate the life-style you wish to pursue during retirement. However, if you have decided not to move from your current location, your life-style will have to accommodate the opportunities provided by that geographic region.

State of citizenship

You can have your cake and eat it too. Many retirees have found that they can save a great deal of money by establishing residency in one state and dividing their time between two or more locations. For example, currently, Texas and Florida do not have income taxes, and thus establishing residency in these states could save Californians, who pay high state income taxes, a great deal of money. Since property taxes are relatively low in Florida and high in Connecticut, a couple who lives in Stanford, Connecticut, might save thousands of dollars by selling their home, purchasing a home in Florida, and renting an apartment in Stanford during those months they want to spend there. Each state has laws governing citizenship and paying taxes, so it will take some careful investigation prior to making a final decision in this matter. However, the final result may well be worth the effort.

What Are Your Retirement Values?

Values. We hear a lot about them today. Almost daily, the news media discusses basic family values, the values of the political right, the values of a cult leader in Texas, and the values of warring factions in the Middle East. Values are basic beliefs that guide our behavior and are our primary source of satisfaction. If our behavior is consistent with the things we believe are important, the probability of being satisfied with our lives is greatly enhanced.

Your values can be satisfied in a variety of life roles. However, before you set off to make major changes in those roles, it is wise to consider what your values are and how they are being satisfied. If you have already retired and are unhappy, the search is a bit different. You are looking for the missing ingredient in your life. What values do you hold that are not being satisfied?

Begin by examining the list of values below and checking which of them you hold.

_____ 1. Adventure—taking risks, doing exciting things

_____ 2. Authority/leadership—being in control, being the boss

_____ 3. Helping others—assisting others with a variety of problems, including education and health care

_____ 4. Autonomy—being independent, making your own decisions

_____ 5. Physical activity—being physically active

_____ 6. Proficiency—performing tasks in an ordered, efficient manner

_____ 7. Intellectual stimulation—performing intellectually stimulating tasks

_____ 8. Working with your hands—using your hands to build/repair/groom/improve things

_____ 9. Solitude—being alone with your own thoughts

_____ 10. Change—having variety in your life

_____ 11. Creativity—being original and creative

_____ 12. Performing—entertaining others

_____ 13. Affiliation—being involved with and accepted by others/belonging

_____ 14. Spirituality—acting on your spiritual beliefs in worship and daily activities

_____ 15. Materialism—pursuing and accumulating material rewards such as money/property

_____ 16. Status—being recognized for your accomplishments

Now that you have completed the checklist, you need to rank these items in terms of their importance to you. Begin to do this by answering these questions:

1. The most important sources of satisfaction in my life are _____

_____

2. If I had to give up one or two aspects of my life, I would give up _____

3. As I look at my life today, it would be hardest to give up

_____

4. I admire other people who have _____

5. I believe that people secretly admire me for _____

6. I get complimented for _____

7. I would most like to be recognized for my _____

Is there a theme that appears in your answers? We tend to be proudest of those accomplishments and activities that reflect our values. If we value helping others and we believe we have done a good job, we appreciate being recognized for our work in helping people. Sometimes, because we tend to excel in those areas that we value, we receive compliments for our performance in those areas. Our secret wishes to be recognized for our accomplishments in a given area are also indicators of our values. Conversely, our willingness to give up an activity demonstrates that we do not value it highly. At this point, identify your three highest life values in the spaces below, beginning with the value that is most important to you and ending with the one that is of third greatest importance. If two values are of equal importance, you may wish to include more than three in this list. In planning your retirement life-style, you should give consideration to roles that will satisfy each of these values.

_____   _____   _____

FIRST   SECOND   THIRD

How are your values being satisfied now?

Each life role has the potential to satisfy many values, depending on how that role is structured. However, the following is a listing of life roles along with the values they are most likely to satisfy. Put a circle around the values you have listed above. For example, if you value affiliation, put a circle around it each time it occurs in the list. If one of your life roles meets one of your values and it is not included in the list, add it and circle it.

Family—helping others; affiliation

Leisure—adventure; solitude and autonomy (individual leisure activities); physical activity; working with hands; affiliation (group leisure activities); performing (unless your occupation involves this activity); creativity; change

Occupation—authority (depending on the nature of your job); materialism; status; intellectual stimulation; proficiency; affiliation (if you work in cooperative group); creativity (some jobs)

Volunteer—helping others; affiliation; change (if you switch activities from time to time)

Community member—spirituality; affiliation; change; helping others; intellectual stimulation

By making a totally honest assessment of your values, you can tell which of the roles you now fill contributes to your overall satisfaction. You can also discover if some of your primary values are not being satisfied: If this is the case, you are likely to feel unfulfilled or even unhappy. You will want to avoid this situation in your retirement life-style by selecting roles carefully.

Creating a retirement life-style

The question that you must answer as you develop a retirement life-style is which roles you can eliminate, add, shrink, or increase while ensuring that you will be satisfied with your life. It will be very difficult to be satisfied if you are worried about money, regardless of whether materialism is one of your basic values. If your retirement income will not support your desired life-style, then a retirement career is a necessity. Poor health may reduce or eliminate certain options, but unless your health is very poor, some work and many other activities are open to you. Relocation can add to your options and enhance the likelihood that your life-style will correspond to your values, but relocation is not without costs.

If you do not act on your values in crafting a retirement life-style, it is a virtual certainty that this will be an unhappy portion of your life. The most critical decision in this process is determining whether to continue in your career or choose another occupation. People who value materialism may be able to relish their past accomplishments and enjoy retirement. However, it is more likely that they will be like the Southern California real estate developer who had accumulated millions but, during retirement, missed the adventure of investing and the rewards that resulted. If your job meets your need for affiliation and you no longer have co-workers and cannot find affiliates in other roles, your retirement may be lonely and unfulfilling. If you need intellectual stimulation, the challenges of game shows and crossword puzzles may soon lose their allure and boredom may result.

Conversely, your current job may not be providing the sources of satisfaction that you need, and you may be thinking, perhaps erroneously, that quitting work will solve your problems and life will become more satisfying when you are a retiree. Unquestionably, many jobs decrease autonomy, do not allow us to be creative, and limit the potential for change in our lives. But there are other jobs available to you, and these may allow you to satisfy many of your values.

The question is why do one in three retirees return to some form of work within a year after retirement, and large numbers of people continue to work at some level even when they do not need the money? The answer is that our occupations allow us to satisfy some and perhaps all of our fundamental values. Unless we can find viable substitutes for work in the other roles in our lives, work must be a part of the retirement life-style.

Decisions Revisited

Earlier it was suggested that you use your imagination to think about the scenarios of your future. It is literally the case that you have the power to create your own future. It is also the case that your future will occur regardless of what you do about it. The only question is do you want your future to be shaped by your own decisions or by the winds of chance? Most people choose the former. As has been noted, fate may already have played a role in the decision-making process if you do not have the money you need to support the life-style you desire. However, think now about your life as it is and how you would like it to be. Then rate the life-style alternatives listed below using a 1 to 5 scale for each criterion listed. If the life-style listed fully meets the criterion, then it should be rated as a 5. If it doesn't meet it at all, then it should receive a rating of 1.

Work–Work–Work

_____ 1. Satisfies my values

_____ 2. Allows me to live where I want

_____ 3. Satisfies my need for money

_____ 4. Is possible given my health

_____ 5. Provides the balance I want among my life roles

_____ 6. Is acceptable to both spouses if applicable

_____ Total Points

Work–Play–Other

_____ 1. Satisfies my values

_____ 2. Allows me to live where I want

_____ 3. Satisfies my need for money

_____ 4. Is possible given my health

_____ 5. Provides the balance I want among my life roles

_____ 6. Is acceptable to both spouses if applicable

_____ Total Points

Volunteer–Play–Other

_____ 1. Satisfies my values

_____ 2. Allows me to live where I want

_____ 3. Satisfies my need for money

_____ 4. Is possible given my health

_____ 5. Provides the balance I want among my life roles

_____ 6. Is acceptable to both spouses (if applicable)

_____ Total Points

Play–Play–Other   _____ 1. Satisfies my values

_____ 2. Allows me to live where I want

_____ 3. Satisfies my need for money

_____ 4. Is possible given my health

_____ 5. Provides the balance I want among my life roles

_____ 6. Is acceptable to both spouses

_____ Total Points

Obviously you are unable to fully predict the future, but if you understand your own values and consider key factors in your life, such as your spouse and your family, you can avoid the disastrous mistakes made by millions of retirees.

Summary   The choice of a retirement life-style ranks among the most important life decisions you have ever made. It will determine your economic, social, and psychological well-being and thus deserves a great deal of your time and attention. If you are already retired, several barriers may arise as you plan, not the least of which is a degree of pessimism about your ability to control your future. Remember, your future will happen regardless of whether you plan.

If is far more likely that you will be too optimistic about your future as a retiree and neglect to plan because you are influenced by the stereotype of an idyllic life. Don't be fooled by stereotypes. Retirees who are happy didn't get to that state by happenstance.

It is entirely possible that you are unsure which would be the best life-style for you at this point. If that is the case, start by interviewing people like yourself who have made the transition to a fulfilling life-style successfully. The more people you talk to, the better you will understand what lies in wait for you as you make the change to retiree, with or without a new career.

Where Will The Retirement Jobs Be?

Did you know that if you had to look at one industry that will produce the most new jobs in the next decade, you would need to look no further than health care?

As previous chapters have noted, the retiree essentially has three choices: to pursue a life of leisure, to go to work for pay, or to pursue a career as a volunteer. If you decide to pursue paid employment, you may wish to start your own business or work full- or part-time for others. In the next chapter, the matter of starting your own business will be discussed in detail, and a wide variety of business opportunities presented. In this chapter, jobs that involve working for others will be considered. First, we will look at jobs that offer employment potential. Then we will see how leisure activities can turn into jobs. In the final section of the chapter, the most rapidly expanding type of job in the labor market will be highlighted: the temporary worker.

One not so secret aspect of the job hunt is to look where the jobs are. In some instances, this means looking in different geographic locations. However, in this chapter, the focus is not on geographic location but rather on occupations that, either because of replacement needs or rapid growth, provide opportunities to workers who have retired (or have been retired) and wish to return to the labor force. First, this chapter will identify occupations that will provide the greatest opportunities for employment in the next 10 to 15 years, particularly focusing on those occupations that can be entered with less than a college degree; many retirees will be unwilling to pursue extensive amounts of additional education and training to make themselves competitive in the labor market.

Some retirees will want to go to law school and hang out a shingle, but law school takes three years, and by the time a new graduate passes the bar and is established, the elapsed time period is likely to be four or more years. Few retirees will want to pursue jobs that require four or more years of additional training. Rather, they will opt for job opportunities that require shorter training periods and may, in fact, enable them to make more money than a lawyer just beginning a practice. However, retirees should not eliminate the option to pursue a career that requires further education totally, particularly if this is the culmination of a life-long fantasy. Recently, the most outstanding "young lawyer" in the Philadelphia area was a 63-year-old woman who had entered law school at the age of 57.

Sex-Role Stereotyping and Your Career

Many retirees grew up in an era when men took men's jobs and women took women's jobs. Men were managers and business owners, and women were teachers and nurses. In today's working world, those stereotypes are not only invalid, they are extremely limiting. Women have always been more willing than men to step across gender boundaries into male-dominated occupations. These incursions into the "territory" of the opposite sex are encouraged. Why? Because in many instances, workers can enhance the chances they will be employed by preparing for and seeking jobs that are dominated by the opposite sex. This is because the hiring policies of the nineties are oriented toward creating a gender balance in the workplace, and often there is much less competition for a job if you are a male seeking employment in a female-dominated occupation. Of course, the opposite is true as well.

The Ticking Clock

All job hunters have a ticking clock. That clock is typically related to the time period in which they hope to secure employment. For young workers who are being supported by their families, this clock may be ticking quite slowly in relative terms. For the retiree who has a decent retirement income and no economic demands to get a job, the clock may be ticking quite slowly. However, for retirees there is another dimension of the clock that must receive attention: their age. Your age at the time you begin the search for a retirement career may determine whether you are willing to engage in a short or long period of training and how much time you can spend deliberating about alternatives and the availability of jobs to you. Federal legislation prohibits discrimination against older workers, defined as people who are older than 40. The reality is that certain types of jobs may be less available to older workers unless they are able to convince employers that they have unique contributions to make, a topic that will be discussed in more detail in the job hunt sections of this book. You must consider the ticking clock as you think about which career you would like to pursue.

The "Romance" of Choosing a New Job

There is one notion that is as phony as a romance novel: follow your heart, and you will have great success in any job you choose. Dozens of career exploration books have been written giving job seekers idealistic suggestions about choosing jobs. One author allows that if you do what you love, the money will follow. A retiree who has a good retirement income can do what he or she loves and not worry whether there is a market for her or his products or services. One retiree filled his workshop with carefully crafted animals and barely sold enough to pay for materials. He loved woodworking, but the public either didn't love his product or he didn't market it well. Another retiree who fancied herself to be a painter filled her house and her garage with her "masterpieces" and, despite her efforts, never sold one painting because her work was so poor.

Another romantic idea is that all you have to do is uncover the so-called "hidden job market," and you will sail into successful employment. This so-called hidden job market is created because major corporations hire from within and therefore never advertise their job vacancies. They do occasionally hire from the outside, but not until they have exhausted the potential employees inside. Most of these corporations have explicit policies that preclude hiring outside people. Hiring from the outside takes approval from the highest levels of management. Most new hires come into corporations at the lowest level as management trainees, secretaries, technicians, and engineers. They then apply for job openings that become available.

Many books provide dozens of clues for uncovering the hidden job market and, once this is accomplished, converting hidden desires into a dream career. These books even suggest that simply by manipulating your resume you can convince unsuspecting personnel managers that your years of handling the household budget is the same as budgeting for a small corporation.

These are both nice ideas—erroneous—but nice. However, identifying the right job for you and then getting that job is not a romantic process. Rather, it is a process that must be grounded in the harsh realities of the workplace of the nineties. Those realities are that we are undergoing a fundamental restructuring of our economy, the result of which is that many jobs are being eliminated while others are being created. These changes are being driven by an aging population, increasing multiculturalism in our society, women's assuming a place of equality, and a global economy that dictates that businesses must compete or die. A job search can be a highly rewarding process, but if it is taken lightly or entered into naively, it can be one of the most punishing life experiences.

It is estimated that there are in excess of one million discouraged workers in the labor force. These are people who have been so unsuccessful in their job searches that they have simply stopped looking. To avoid this situation, you must carefully consider all your options, not just those that seem most appealing or those you have entertained in your fantasies.

High Probability vs. Low Probability Jobs

Intuitively, every job searcher understands that the likelihood of getting different types of jobs varies. The headlines in local newspapers tell us that there is a shortage of qualified nurses, and the help-wanted ads in those same papers verify the headline. A person who has a degree in nursing is involved in a high probability job search. On the other hand, unskilled laborers who are displaced by computers are likely to engage in a low probability job search if they pursue similar jobs. The trick is to identify and pursue jobs that offer a high probability of success.

The first step toward a high probability job search is to identify occupations that offer likely opportunities for employment. Let's look at two promising careers that can be prepared for with two years or less of education. It is projected that in the next 15 years the number of paralegals, people who are trained to assist lawyers in conducting research and performing other legal tasks, will grow by 85 percent. This growth rate makes it the fastest growing occupation requiring less than a four-year college degree. Currently, there are about 90,000 paralegals in the labor market, so by 2005 the number will be 167,000, an increase of 77,000. In contrast, there will be only a 42-percent growth rate in the number of licensed practical nurses (LPNs). However, there are currently 527,000 LPNs at work, and a 42-percent increase translates to a numerical increase of a whopping 269,000 new jobs. Moreover, because of retirements and shifts in employment, many more LPNs will be needed during the coming years. The moral is simple: one way that retirees can maximize their chances of successfully finding a job is to consider the total number of job vacancies and not be misled by figures such as the expected percent of increase.

I am not suggesting that under no circumstances should a retiree pursue what I term low probability occupational job searches. I am suggesting that if the retiree elects to pursue careers in occupations where there are limited opportunities, two outcomes may result. First, it is likely that it may take more time to find a job, depending upon the number and qualifications of other job hunters. Second, there is a greater likelihood of failure, that is, no job will be found. Retirees need to consider what their tolerance for failure is and how long they can afford to engage in a job search before they begin.

High Probability Careers

High probability careers can be divided into three groups based upon the amount of training or education they require. Table 3.1 is a listing of occupations that are expected to grow rapidly in the next decade and beyond. As you examine this table, circle jobs that might be of interest to you.

TABLE 3.1

Occupations With The Largest Increase In Numbers To 2005

Education Requirements	# Jobs Now	# New Jobs	Weekly Salary
MINIMUM OF COLLEGE DEGREE			
Systems analysts and computer scientists*	463,000	366,000	$700
Physical therapists	88,000	67,000	550
Operations research analysts	57,000	42,000	600
Psychologists (master's degree)	125,000	82,000	500
Computer programmers*	565,000	317,000	500
Occupational therapists	36,000	20,000	510
Management analysts	151,000	79,000	600
Public relations managers	427,000	203,000	400
General managers/top executives*	3,086,000	598,000	700 & up
Teachers elementary and secondary*	2,528,000	800,000	450
Accountants and auditors*	985,000	340,000	500
Lawyers*	587,000	206,000	550
SOME POSTSECONDARY TRAINING OR EXTENSIVE ON-THE-JOB TRAINING			
Paralegals	90,000	77,000	400
Radiologic technicians	145,000	104,000	430
Medical assistants	165,000	122,000	280
Physical therapy aides	35,000	29,000	280
Data processing equipment repairers	84,000	50,000	450
Medical records technicians	52,000	28,000	350
Surgical technicians	38,000	21,000	400
Cooks, restaurants*	615,000	257,000	270
Respiratory therapists	60,000	31,000	450
Licensed practical nurses*	527,000	269,000	300
Maintenance workers	1,128,000	251,000	250
Teacher aides*	808,000	278,000	245

TABLE 3.1 continued

Education Requirements	# Jobs Now	# New Jobs	Weekly Salary
Registered nurses*	1,727,000	767,000	500
Legal secretaries	281,000	133,000	300
Medical secretaries	232,000	158,000	300
HIGH SCHOOL OR LESS			
Home health aides*	287,000	263,000	200
Home care aides	88,000	67,000	200
Human services workers	145,000	103,000	250
Correction officers	230,000	142,000	350
Travel agents	132,000	82,000	250
Flight attendants	101,000	59,000	250
Sales persons, retail*	3,619,000	887,000	200
Clerks*	3,875,000	676,000	220
Cashiers*	2,633,000	685,000	200
Food counter workers*	1,607,000	550,000	200
Truck drivers*	2,362,000	617,000	480
Nurse's aides/orderlies*	1,274,000	552,000	250
Janitors/cleaners*	3,007,000	555,000	225
Waiters/waitresses*		449,000	100**
Food preparation workers	1,156,000	365,000	170
Receptionists*	900,000	422,000	250
Gardeners/grounds keepers*	874,000	348,000	250
Guards*	883,000	298,000	250
Child care workers	725,000	353,000	175
Secretaries*	3,064,000	248,000	300
Cooks, short order*	743,000	246,000	200
Clerical supervisors*	1,218,000	263,000	325
Stock clerks*	1,242,000	209,000	200

*These jobs will produce almost 50 percent of the growth among all jobs. (Occupational Outlook Quarterly, Fall, 1991).

Go back to those jobs that you have circled and select two or three that may be of interest to you. List them here.

1. _____

2. _____

3. _____

Self-Employment   It has been well documented that the vast majority of jobs in this country are being created by small businesses, a trend that will be taken up in more detail in the next chapter. However, in table 3.2 the self-employment occupations that are growing the fastest are listed. Place a circle around any of these jobs that may be of interest to you.

TABLE 3.2

Leading Growth Self-Employment Jobs

Job	Projected New Jobs
1. Food service and lodging managers	450,000
2. Cleaners, household and industrial	225,000
3. Child care workers	210,000
4. Hairdressers and cosmetologists	154,000
5. Writers, artists, and entertainers	86,000
6. Carpenters	77,000
7. Painters and paperhangers	75,000
8. Accountants and auditors	58,000
9. Psychologists	39,000
10. Property and real estate managers	33,000
11. Management analysts	32,000
12. Instructors	27,000
13. Real estate brokers/appraisers	26,000
14. Real estate sales	21,000
15. Electricians	17,000

Eventually you will have to decide whether to become self-employed. However, for now go back to table 3.2 and select the two or three jobs that are of the greatest interest to you and list them here.

1. _____

2. _____

3. _____

Jobs that are declining in number

Table 3.1 depicts areas where large numbers of jobs will be available in the years ahead. In table 3.3, the jobs that will show the greatest decline in numbers are listed. In launching your high probability job search, should you consider an occupation where numbers are actually declining? Let's take a look at the jobs before answering this question.

TABLE 3.3

Jobs That Will Decline The Most

Job	*Jobs Lost*
1. Bookkeeping and accounting clerks	133,000
2. Child care workers, private	124,000
3. Sewing machine operators, garment	116,000
4. Electrical/electronics assemblers	186,000*
5. Typists and word processors	103,000
6. Private household workers	101,000
7. Farm workers	92,000
8. Textile machine operators	61,000
9. Switchboard operators	57,000
10. Machine operators	112,000*
11. Installers and repairers	96,000*
12. Central office operators	31,000
13. Statistical clerks	31,000
14. Bank tellers	25,000
15. Service station attendants	17,000
16. Director assistance operators	16,000
17. Butchers and meat cutters	14,000
18. Meter readers, utilities	12,000

*includes two categories of jobs

Although these jobs are declining rapidly, many of them still offer opportunities for employment simply because they comprise such a large segment of the labor force. For example, there are currently more than 500,000 bank tellers working in this country, many of whom work part-time. Similarly, there are approximately 1.5 million typists and word processors currently employed, and because of attrition, many will be needed in the future. This same statement can be made for the various types of clerks in the labor market. Currently there are in excess of 15 million clerks of various types in the work force, and the loss of 150,000 jobs in some of the subtypes of clerks over the next decade does not take away from the fact that this occupation offers great opportunities for employment. On the other hand, the number of private household workers will shrink from about 750,000 to 650,000 in the near future, a considerable decline. The bottom line: don't be misled by newspaper articles that tell you a particular occupation is declining. It may very well provide you with the right type of opportunity. Go back to table 3.3 and identify any jobs that warrant further investigation. List those jobs here.

1. _____

2. _____

3. _____

Perhaps you noted that the decline in private household workers is accompanied by an increase of 225,000 cleaners, private and industrial (see table 3.3). What's going on? Isn't this double talk? No, what we are seeing is a fundamental shift in the way that households and businesses get cleaned: they contract with independent businesses. The implication is simple. If you want to get into the cleaning area, open a business and go after the emerging market.

Growth industries   Another way to look at where the jobs are is to look at projections of growth for various industries. Because over 80 percent of the jobs in the United States fall into the service sector (as opposed to the production or manufacture of goods), I will focus on those industries that offer services since they will continue to grow and those that produce products will decline. As can be seen in table 3.4, certain service industries, particularly health care, will boom in the years ahead. As you examine table 3.4, make notes in the margins if you have any experience, expertise, or interest in any of these industries.

TABLE 3.4

Service Industries That Will Grow In The Nineties

Industry	Growth in Jobs (Millions)
1. Health care	3.9
• This is a huge industry with 9 million workers	
• One out of six new jobs will be in this industry	
• Most jobs require less than a B.S.	
• Part-time work is available	
2. Business services	2.4
• Computer and data processing services will be in particular demand	
• Management consulting, public relations, and advertising services also in demand	
• Specialized training a must	
• Wages higher than others	
3. Education	2.3
• Largest employer—9.5 million jobs	
• Job openings for teachers will increase, primarily because of replacement needs.	
4. Engineering and management	1.3
• Most jobs require two years or more in training	
• Technical consultation services in demand	
• Jobs relatively high paying	
• Technician jobs most prevalent	
5. Social services	1.1
• Rapidly growing industry	
• Average earnings lower than other fields	
• Must want to help others to enjoy this work	
• Many of the new openings will be service as opposed to professional jobs, but the demand in both areas remains strong	
6. Hotels	.5
• Plentiful opportunities for part-time work	
• Many jobs require no training or experience	
• Workplace is small in most instances	
• About 20 percent of workers are self-employed	
• Retirees are welcome	
7. Legal services	.3
• Number of jobs will grow rapidly	
• Various jobs will be available	
• Paralegals and legal secretaries will be in demand	
8. Amusement and recreation	.3
• Jobs will grow rapidly	
• Many jobs require no training	
• Wide variety of occupations available	
• Part-time job opportunities	
9. Auto repair and related, including rental	.3
• Many jobs require relatively short training periods	
• Self-employment opportunities will be available	
10. Personal services	.2
• Additions will be in administrative support and health-related jobs	
• Part-time work available	
• Average earnings are relatively low	

At this time which, if any, of these industries are of greatest interest to you? _____

_____

Can you identify any specific jobs that might be available to you in these industries? If you can, make a note of these at this time.

1. _____

2. _____

3. _____

Hobbies to Careers

Almost everyone has had the fantasy from time to time of turning the activity that they enjoy most into a career. Many times retirees have this opportunity. I have just identified the jobs and industries that offer the most opportunities for workers currently and in the future. Now I want to turn to identifying hobbies that may have career implications. In a few instances, hobbies can be converted directly into careers. A person who is a skilled carpenter can often take that skill to the job market and cash in. However, most people's hobbies only point the way to job options. They do not translate directly to career options. In order for those options to become reality, additional training may be required. Keep in mind throughout this discussion that no matter how much you enjoy something, someone else has to want the service or product that results from your efforts. What follows is a series of tables that list many common hobbies and the types of jobs that may be related to these hobbies. If you pursue any of these hobbies, place circles around associated jobs that may be of interest to you as you read through the list.

TABLE 3.5

Hobbies and Related Jobs

ARTISTIC ACTIVITIES

Acting in an amateur play or production

- Drama teacher
- Actor
- Mime

Announcer at various events

- Radio/TV announcer

Make-up artist at amateur events

- Cosmetologist/barber
- Make-up artist
- Sales representative for cosmetic firm
- Pet groomer (for hair specialists)

Cake decorator

- Cake decorator–bakery
- Caterer

Constructing/designing sets for amateur events

- Furniture designer/repairer
- Interior designer
- Set designer–television, motion pictures

Costume design for amateur events

- Clothing designer, including accessories
- Clothing repairer
- Classic clothing store operator
- Used clothing store manager

Dance instructor

- Dance instructor
- Choreographer

Designing own greeting cards

- Greeting card designer
- Merchandiser
- Card shop manager

Flower arranging

- Floral designer
- Flower shop operator
- Nursery sales or operator

Leather work

- Furniture upholsterer
- Saddle maker
- Harness repairer
- Book binder

Magic tricks

- Entertainer/magician
- Emcee
- Greeter/host/hospitality services

Modeling

- Model
- Arranging fashion shows

Needle work

- Crafts sales
- Clothing repairer

Playing musical instrument

- Musician
- Instructor
- Music teacher

Sketching

- Fashion artist
- Quick sketch artist in amusement area
- Cartoonist
- Illustrator
- Window designer

Writing, prose

- Book editor
- Nonfiction writer
- Copy editor–newspaper
- Free-lance writer

Song writing

- Jingle writer for advertising firm
- Editor
- Song writer
- Booking agent for musical groups

SCIENTIFIC/MATHEMATICAL ACTIVITIES

Breeding animals

- Purebred animal breeder
- Pet boarding kennel operator
- Veterinarian technician
- Animal trainer

Experiment with plants

- Nursery or greenhouse worker/manager
- Landscaper
- Greens keeper—golf course or other sports facilities

TABLE 3.5 continued

- Lawn manager
- Gardener
- Tree surgeon

Help friends with taxes
- Tax preparer (e.g., H & R Block)
- Accountant
- Auditor
- Bookkeeper

Read medical/scientific journals
- Medical technician/technologist
- Scientific technician/technologist
- Engineering technician
- Laboratory technician
- Quality control technician

SECURITY AND LAW ENFORCEMENT ACTIVITIES

Directing traffic at school and neighborhood events
- Gate guard at airports, parking lots
- Traffic technician
- Parking analyst
- Accident prevention squad
- Parking enforcement operator

Organizing community watch
- Airline security officer
- Department store security officer
- Energy use controller
- Pollution controller
- Security services business owner

- Building inspector
- Fire marshall/inspector

Reading detective novels/watching detective shows on television
- Armored car driver
- Dispatcher in police station
- Police officer
- Mortgage loan processor
- Claims clerk or adjustor–insurance
- Jailer
- Corrections officer
- Repossessor
- Airlines security officer

MECHANICAL/CONSTRUCTION ACTIVITIES

Appliance repair
- Small appliance repairer
- Appliance sales

Electrical equipment repair
- Electronics technician
- Electrician
- VCR repairer
- Electrical motor repairer

Construction projects
- Carpenter
- Cabinet builder
- Kitchen appliance installer
- Tile setter
- Mason
- Plumber
- Furniture builder and repairer

Sketching machines and equipment
- Drafter
- Engineering technician

Equipment/auto maintenance
- Auto mechanic
- Small engine repairer
- Bicycle repairer
- Motorcycle repairer

Gun repair
- Gunsmith
- Hunting/fishing store operator

HELPING/SERVICE ACTIVITIES

Coaching children and adults
- Recreation director/coordinator
- Umpire/referee

Chauffering
- Bus driver
- Taxi driver
- Ambulance driver

Conducting physical activities or exercise programs for the elderly or disabled
- Physical therapist
- Occupational therapist
- Recreational therapist
- Aides for therapists

Cooking for large groups
- Restaurant owner
- Cook/chef

Developing ads/sales activities for clubs and organizations or selling ads for organizations
- Direct mail sales
- Advertising clerk
- Sales clerk/associate

TABLE 3.5 continued

First aid worker/instructor

- Nurse
- Emergency medical technician
- Child care worker
- Nursing home attendant
- Home health aide
- Nurse's aide/orderly
- Human resources worker

Planning or organizing school or community organization activities

- Coordinator of social services
- Human resources worker

Setting tables for community organizations

- Waiter/waitress
- Host/hostess

Serving as secretary or treasurer of community group

- Secretary
- Bookkeeper
- Clerical supervisor

Tutoring/teaching

- Teacher

- Teacher aide
- Adult education instructor

Volunteering in hospitals, youth camps, fire departments

- Nursery school worker
- Teacher aide
- Fire fighter
- Host/hostess

CLERICAL ACTIVITIES

Operating business machines as volunteer

- Computer operator
- Peripheral machine operator
- Typist/word processor

Routine clerical activities

- Correspondence clerk
- Court stenographer
- Scheduler/meeting coordinator

Record keeping

- Bookkeeper
- Medical records technician
- Librarian/aide

LEADERSHIP ACTIVITIES AND ASSOCIATED JOBS

Public speaking

- Receptionist
- Hospitality services
- Sales—all types
- Tourist information clerk
- Chamber of commerce representative
- Loan collector

Political campaign aide

- Sales
- Claims adjuster
- Personnel recruiter
- Development officer/fund raiser

Membership chair

- Advertising agency worker
- Sales representative

President

- Insurance sales
- Broker
- Commission sales
- Supervisory position

This is obviously only a partial list. If none of the leisure activities listed correspond to the one you enjoy, start by listing the activity that you enjoy the most and brainstorm about types of jobs associated with it. One way to do this is to consider where you buy goods or services for your hobby. For example, if your hobby is sewing, you undoubtedly frequent some fabric shops to purchase supplies and equipment. You may also make things for other people if you are talented. If you fish, you purchase bait and tackle at a minimum. You may also own a boat, have to get it repaired from time to time, and have a variety of equipment associated with the boat that has to be maintained. You may also employ a guide to take you on fishing expeditions. All of these ideas suggest possible occupations, ranging from operating a fabric shop to booking fishing expeditions.

Now make a list of your hobbies and leisure activities, starting with the one that you enjoy the most. Then think of all the jobs associated with your hobby. Are any of them of interest to you? Have you noticed jobs that could be done better? Cheaper? That would serve a different clientele? For example, the number of golfers will grow rapidly in the next decade, according to all projections. However, the really untapped market in this area is women. Hundreds, and perhaps thousands, of people are trying to figure out how to tap this market for shoes, clubs, lessons, and golf tour packages.

At this point, make a list of two or three job ideas that you selected from the table or from thinking about your hobbies that you would like to explore further.

1. _____

2. _____

3. _____

If You Want To Do It, You Can—As A Temporary

One of the results of the restructuring of the labor force in the eighties is the increase in the number of temporary jobs. Businesses are reluctant to take on full-time employees because they are concerned about fringe benefits costs, do not like the problems associated with furloughing or dismissing employees, and increasingly realize that they must be flexible enough to deal with rapidly changing business conditions. The result: temporary jobs are the fastest-growing jobs in the labor force.

At one time, temporary jobs were confined to clerical workers such as secretaries and clerks. Now temporary jobs from all occupational groups are available. For example, there are agencies that place physicians; lawyers; dentists; engineers; accountants and auditors; nurses; nurse's aides and orderlies; janitors and cleaners; programmers; writers; and, of course, clerical workers, including word processors, computer operators, secretaries, and clerks. Moreover, an agency may provide a variety of different temporary workers. One agency advertised temporaries in the following areas:

Word processors	Typists
Executive secretaries	Bookkeepers
Legal secretaries	Tellers
Transcriptionists	Telemarketers
Customer services	Assemblers
Receptionists	Material handlers
Accounting clerks	Landscapers
General office clerks	Distribution clerks
Records clerks	Merchandisers
Demonstrators	Accountants
Data entry clerks	Engineers
Programmers	Systems analysts
Computer operators	Quality control technicians

Another agency was a bit more specialized. It offered unique temporary workers.

Belly dancers	Star impersonators
Strippers	Clowns
Comedy routines	Magicians
Singing telegrams	Mini-carnivals
Gag gift shows	

The temporary job may be the perfect opportunity for retired professionals who would like to "keep their hand in" but do not wish to maintain an office and a full-time practice. Temporary offices are also willing to provide training in many instances, and so the person who wishes to move into a new field may be able to do so through a temporary agency. The good news is that the temporary agency provides the person who wishes to work part-time with the perfect job. Workers simply specify how much they are willing to work, and the agency does the rest. The bad news is that, in many instances, the agency provides no fringe benefits. For some retirees this will not be a problem, because they were vested in health plans in the jobs from which they retired. For others this will be a barrier to becoming a temporary worker.

Many workers use temporary agencies as a way to locate a permanent job. Temporaries are frequently hired to fill unexpected vacancies, and if the temporary does a good job, he or she can be the number-one candidate to fill the position. In order to get more information about opportunities to work as a temporary, check the classified advertisement in your local telephone book. You may need to look in several locations to get a complete picture. Health care professionals may be listed under "nursing" or "health care." Other listings can be found under "employment contractors" or "temporary health care." A relatively complete listing of temporary agencies is available from the National Association of Temporary Services, 119 South Saint Asaph Street, Alexandria, VA 22314, for the pricey cost of $150 plus handling and postage.

At some point, you will have to decide whether to work full- or part-time. You do not have to make that decision now, but one of your considerations in making your final decision may well be whether temporary employment is available in your area.

Your Values and Jobs

In chapter 2 it was suggested that you should consider your values when selecting a retirement life-style. That same advice holds when selecting a retirement career. What follows is a listing of the same values that appeared in that chapter and some promising occupations that will fulfill those values. The best approach to accessing this list is to circle jobs of interest that seem to correspond to your values.

TABLE 3.6

Work Values And Occupations That Will Satisfy Them

- **Adventure**

  Law enforcement officer

  Fire fighter

  Greens keeper

  Dog catcher

  Correction officer

  Security consultant

  Guard

- **Helping others**

  YMCA/YWCA director

  Social service aide

  Physical therapist and aides

  Emergency medical technician

  Medical assistant

- **Physical activity**

  Umpire/referee

  Heavy equipment operator

  Waiter/waitress

  Repairers, all types

  Construction trades

- **Intellectual stimulation**

  Engineering technologist

  Copywriter

  Editor

  Food technologist

  Creative writer

- **Solitude**

  Stock clerk

  Warehouse worker

  Truck driver, long distance

  Gardener, truck

  Research technician

- **Authority/Leadership**

  Theater stage manager

  Tree surgeon

  Supervisor

  Teacher

  Bank examiner

  Dietician

  Government inspector

- **Autonomy**

  Small business owner

  Caterer

  Manager, sports facility

  Hotel/motel manager

  Credit manager

- **Proficiency**

  Bookkeeper

  Medical technician

  Dispatcher

  Electronics technician

  Proofreader

- **Working with hands**

  Barber

  Carpenter

  Mechanic

  Clothes designer

  Tailor/seamstress

- **Change**

  Sales representative

  Business manager

  Chamber of commerce worker

  Development officer

  Coordinator/volunteer

TABLE 3.6 continued

- **Creativity**

  Art teacher/instructor

  Floral designer

  Illustrator, technical

  Auctioneer

  Telemarketer

- **Affiliation**

  Usher

  Nurses aide/orderly

  Flight attendant

  Dietary aide

  Teacher aide

- **Materialism**

  Car sales

  Insurance agent

  Travel agent

  Business owner

  Manager

- **Performing**

  Mime

  Musician

  Singer

  Emcee/host

  Announcer

- **Spirituality**

  Bookstore owner (religious material)

  Church superintendent

  Bible sales

  Evangelist

- **Status**

  Finance officer

  Physician's assistant

  Public relations worker

  Lawyer/paralegal

  Assignments editor, TV

Now go back and pick two or three jobs from this list that you would like to explore in greater detail.

1. _____

2. _____

3. _____

Putting It Together   At this point it is time to make some preliminary decisions. You have been exposed to over 100 high probability careers, the 10 fastest-growing industries, 175 careers that can be related to various hobbies, and over 80 occupations that can satisfy 16 different values. With a few exceptions, these careers are open to you with a reasonable amount of retraining or experience. Of course, as I mentioned at the outset, if you want to be a lawyer or other professional that requires extensive training, go for it! You should have identified at least a few jobs that have some appeal to you.

If you are considering whether to start your own business, you'll want to wait until you read the next chapter. If you are considering volunteering, you may want to wait until you have read the next two chapters. However, if you do not want to be self-employed, but you do want to work, look back at the alternatives you have listed and select one or two for in-depth exploration. To do this, take the following steps.

1. Talk to two or three people who are engaged in each career. Ask them what they do and do not like about the job, how much money people in that job in your area earn as beginners, and what kind of training and experience a worker needs.

2. Follow around a person employed in the occupations you are interested in for a few days, or be an unpaid volunteer for a week. Even better, try to get a part-time job in your field of interest.

3. Read the *Occupational Outlook Handbook* to get a better idea about the job, working conditions, salary, and supply and demand. This book should be available in your local library. If not, visit a local community college or university. The career placement center will have a copy, and so will most high school counseling and guidance programs.

4. If retraining is required, talk to someone, such as a career counselor at a community college or vocational technical school, about the nature, length, and cost of the training.

5. Talk over the working conditions and hours with your spouse or significant other. Try to determine if the job will interfere with your retirement life-style.

6. Visit or call your local employment office (Job Service). Ask about opportunities in the field you are considering. Also talk to the placement officer at the training institution you are considering. Find out if graduates of the program you are considering get

jobs. Ask about the special problems people of your age may have being employed in that area.

7. If you have decided that you have the needed qualifications to fill the job of interest to you, proceed to the job hunt section in this book.

Summary   The American labor market has changed dramatically in the last 20 years, but it still provides great numbers of opportunities for people willing to explore the possibilities. I have recommended that you embark upon what I term a high probability job search, which means looking for jobs in occupations with rapidly expanding opportunities or in occupations that employ large numbers of people with high turnover rates. No matter how great your job-hunting skills are, unless there are job openings, you will be unsuccessful. In the final analysis, you need to consider your local situation, because the availability of jobs varies tremendously in different geographic locations. You may also wish to consider relocation as a possibility in your search for a new career.

Unless you are absolutely desperate, you should never choose a job on the basis of availability. Jobs can be positive and uplifting or painful and unhappy. You should choose a job that matches your values, interests, and chosen life-style.

Starting Your
Own Business

*Did you know that 85 percent of all new jobs in this
country are being created by small businesses?*

***Ask Not for Whom the
Business Bell Tolls***

Many people spend their lives dreaming of starting their
own businesses. What better time is there to act on this
dream than when you have left your job and are casting
about for something to do? Starting your own business
eliminates the job hunt, but it starts you on an entirely different type of search: finding the right business for you.

The Good News—and the Bad

If you are actively considering starting your own business, there is much good news. Every expert on the future of the labor market agrees that there has never been a better time to start a business than the present. But there is some bad news as well. The bad news is that only about 50 percent of all small businesses survive five years or more. However, you can dramatically alter those odds if you plan carefully. Besides the risks, there are some other considerations. Starting a business can take tremendous amounts of time and energy and typically requires the entrepreneur to risk some money. Perhaps the best advice that can be given to you if you are interested in starting a business is to carefully assess your motivation, determination, risk-taking ability, and the amount of perspiration you are willing to shed.

What? Me? An Entrepreneur?

If you have been working for others and are now considering becoming an entrepreneur, it may be time to check your entrepreneurial pulse. David Robinson, author of *What Is an Entrepreneur?* defines an *entrepreneur* as one who is involved in the business of selling, trading, or making things. Typically, entrepreneurs are the captains of their own ships; that is, they are involved in what are termed *sole proprietorships,* although they may take on partners if the situation warrants. Robinson suggests that the aim of the entrepreneur is to increase his or her influence and wealth. In other words, entrepreneurs do not start businesses just to pass the time.

Robinson cites the work of John G. Burch, who described the personality traits of the entrepreneur as having a need to achieve and be rewarded for that achievement; valuing hard work; valuing business gains; willing, perhaps eager, to accept responsibility; valuing excellence; and being optimistic in nature. Burch also suggests that entrepreneurs are intuitive in nature; that is, they act on their instincts and hunches. To this list of characteristics must be added the propensity for risk taking. Entrepreneurs are able to recognize opportunities and have the courage to act on their instincts. I would suggest that the successful entrepreneur may act in a manner that to some might seem impulsive, but intuition is really nothing more than "clumped cognitions," that is, behavior based upon past learning.

Successful entrepreneurs appear intuitive because they know an area, such as retailing, well. Sam Walton is viewed as a retailing genius, and the term *entrepreneur* certainly comes to mind when we hear his name. However, Sam Walton was well into his career before he established Wal-Mart. Ray Kroc, founder of McDonald's, studied the innovative methods of the McDonald brothers in San Bernardino before he bought the rights to their process. Donald Trump was born into a family that dealt in commercial real estate and admits that he learned much of his deal-making ability early in his life. Kroc and Walton knew how the businesses they started worked and found ways to market them to the public. Walton also knew how the competition functioned and set out to devise more efficient, cheaper ways to market many of the same products they sold. Kroc changed eating habits just as Walton changed retailing. Trump simply applied the principals he had learned early in his life to amass a fortune dealing in real estate.

Trump, Kroc, and Walton, like other entrepreneurs, believed in themselves. Trump, like many entrepreneurs, probably allowed his overabundance of self-confidence to get him into difficulty, but it is undoubtedly the case that his confidence in his own ability has allowed him to persevere in the face of adversity.

You may not have all of the characteristics Burch noted, but you must believe in yourself and your ability to start and nourish a business to success. You may not be opportunistic, but you must have the ability to use data to identify good and bad opportunities. You do not have to be interested in becoming wealthy, but unless you are interested in making money your business will soon languish, for it is profit that drives businesses ahead. Finally, you may not have the propensity for risk taking that would lead you to chance your entire retirement nest egg on opening a business, but some personal, and at times some financial, risk taking is necessary when you begin a business if you are to be successful, because to try in this arena is to risk failure. According to John Burch, if you are dependence seeking, eager to maintain instead of expand your income, nonrisk taking, and overly analytic as opposed to relying on your intuition, you fail the test for entrepreneurship.

Butcher, Baker, or Computer Store Owner?

The first question you must ask is what type of business you are interested in starting. Full-time? Part-time? Service oriented? Making a product? Businesses begin with ideas or concepts, typically because the prospective owner recognizes that a service is not being performed or could be performed cheaper or better. Some also recognize that certain products are either not available or not available at a reasonable cost. Perhaps you don't have an idea or concept at this point; you simply believe that you would like to try your hand at starting a business. Let's look at some possibilities based on the projections of the U.S. Department of Labor and small business experts. One thing to remember is that the list that follows is only meant to stimulate your imagination. The *Business Opportunities Handbook* contains over 2,300 business opportunities, including franchises, mail-order businesses, vending companies, and distributorships. If you add to this list the countless unadvertised business opportunities plus the ideas generated by millions of entrepreneurs, you can easily see why small businesses are popular.

The following businesses can be started on a part-time basis with a minimum of cash. Check any that seem to be interesting to you. I've put some costs of starting these businesses into this section and the next based largely on the estimates of companies that franchise these businesses. However, the person who is about to start a business has many decisions to make that will dramatically influence start-up and operating costs, so don't get greatly involved with costs at this time. More about costs later.

Businesses that can be operated part-time

_____ Pet sitting ($250–500)

_____ Tutoring and coaching services ($250–3,000)

_____ Catering service ($250–10,000)

_____ Burglar alarm installation and maintenance ($15,000–$30,000)

_____ Clothing alterations shop ($200–1,500)

_____ Mediator/dispute settlement ($500–15,000)

_____ Personal shopping service (groceries, clothes) ($500–$1000)

_____ Videographer (weddings, birthday parties) ($1,500–10,000)

_____ Shopping mall booth ($3,500–10,000)

_____ Calligraphy service (wedding invitations, diplomas) ($250–3000)

_____ Driving instructor ($10,000–15,000)

_____ Direct sales (e.g., Mary Kay Cosmetics, Amway, Avon, Tupperware) ($3,000–6,000)

_____ Firewood delivery ($4,000–10,000)

_____ Real estate sales ($2,500–35,000)

_____ Real estate appraisal (residential and commercial) ($500–15,000)

_____ Genealogy service ($500–1000)

_____ Pet grooming ($1,000–5,000)

_____ Furniture repair and antique refinishing ($4,000–15,000)

_____ Appliance repair ($5,000–25,000)

_____ Crafts (leather, quilts, jewelry, stained glass, clock making) ($100–500)

_____ Yard Care ($1,000–15,000)

_____ Computer cleaning service ($3,000–5,000)

Part-time businesses that require higher amounts of start-up capital include:

_____ Laundromat ($125,000–250,000 plus)

_____ Self-storage units ($500,000 plus)

_____ Miniature golf (part-time in colder areas of the country) ($50,000–500,000)

_____ Limousine service ($20,000–120,000)

The following businesses will meet the demands of the nineties and beyond, but they will require you to commit to full-time work. Again, check any that sound interesting.

Businesses that require full-time work

_____ Advertising businesses (direct mail) ($5,000–50,000)

_____ Janitorial services ($2,000–20,000)

_____ Tutoring centers ($50,000–120,000)

_____ Temporary personnel placement services (word processors, accountants, engineers, physicians) ($50,000–140,000)

_____ Day-care centers, including children and seniors ($25,000–250,000)

_____ Security services, including residential and commercial ($150,000–300,000)

_____ In-home health care services ($50,000–375,000)

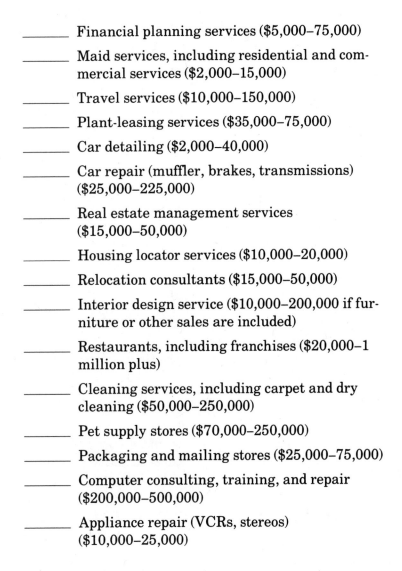

_____ Financial planning services ($5,000–75,000)

_____ Maid services, including residential and commercial services ($2,000–15,000)

_____ Travel services ($10,000–150,000)

_____ Plant-leasing services ($35,000–75,000)

_____ Car detailing ($2,000–40,000)

_____ Car repair (muffler, brakes, transmissions) ($25,000–225,000)

_____ Real estate management services ($15,000–50,000)

_____ Housing locator services ($10,000–20,000)

_____ Relocation consultants ($15,000–50,000)

_____ Interior design service ($10,000–200,000 if furniture or other sales are included)

_____ Restaurants, including franchises ($20,000–1 million plus)

_____ Cleaning services, including carpet and dry cleaning ($50,000–250,000)

_____ Pet supply stores ($70,000–250,000)

_____ Packaging and mailing stores ($25,000–75,000)

_____ Computer consulting, training, and repair ($200,000–500,000)

_____ Appliance repair (VCRs, stereos) ($10,000–25,000)

A Dream Come True—Turning Fun into Profit

Our leisure activities can often be transformed into successful businesses. Ron, who had sailed throughout his working life, now offers luxury sailing cruises to small groups in the Virgin Islands. Lawrence, who had played in a Dixieland Band, became the manager of the band and has bookings in three states. Margaret, who had traveled extensively during her career as a teacher, started organizing tours to the Holy Land at Christmas and Easter at the end of her career. These are only three examples of how hundreds of people have transformed their leisure activities into part-time and full-time activities and related careers. What follows is a listing of leisure activities and retirement businesses that might grow out of them.

Leisure Activity	Possible Business
Artistic activities	teaching music, dance, singing art/music store
Crafts	craft retailer/wholesaler
	furniture manufacturing
	photography studio
Outdoor activities	leisure clothing sales
	fishing, camping/hiking tours
	equipment sales (e.g., tennis)
	fitness camps/retreats
	youth camps
	white water rafting tours
Collecting	antique shop
	antique restoration
	furniture repair
	sports card shops/sales

Are There Really Lands of Opportunity?

Another way to consider where to look for small business opportunities is to notice where these businesses are growing rapidly. Sanitary services, carpentry, masonry, real estate sales and management, credit reporting and collection, computer and data-processing services, mailing services, copying, music stores, engineering and architectural services, and nonresidential construction are some of these industries. The fact is that with few exceptions, a service-oriented economy offers the entrepreneur many opportunities to start successful small businesses.

No Crystal Ball Needed

The editors of *Income Opportunities* suggest that you use the following criteria when deciding which small business is for you: (1) income you desire, (2) whether you enjoy making sales calls (if you don't, stay out of businesses that require it), (3) amount of travel you can tolerate, (4) the schedule you wish to maintain (e.g., total hours, whether you wish to work days, nights, weekends), (4) the arrangements you expect to make for labor (yourself only, family involvement, other employees), (5) whether you enjoy interacting with the public (most small businesses require involvement with people, but a few, such as direct mail advertising services, do not), (6) whether your status in the community is of concern (waste management may make you a bundle, but it won't get you invited to the mayor's house for dinner), and (7) your physical stamina.

Finally You Gotta Choose: Defining the Concept

To reiterate, whether you start with your own concept or choose from the multitude of franchises available, every business starts with an idea. The idea needs to be tested and refined. There are several ways that this can be accomplished. Begin by asking yourself, "How much do I really know about the business that I am interested in starting?" I talked to three bankers who make loans to people interested in starting their own businesses. While they agreed on many things when it came time to make loans to entrepreneurs, the factor that they considered first was the person's knowledge about the product or service and the businesses designed to sell it. They also wanted some assurances, either in the form of hands-on management experience or management training (preferably both), that the person applying for a loan could manage the business he or she was planning. They also wanted some assurances that there was a need for the proposed business, that the business would make money.

David Gumpert, author of *How to Really Start Your Own Business,* suggests that you culminate your search for an idea for a small business by trying to describe what you intend to do in 50 words or less. One person who recently started a tire store in a small town stated his idea as follows:

> I want to immediately start a retail outlet for automobile, truck and tractor tires that will include sales, tire installation and repairs, tire balancing, and front-end alignment. Within a year I want to add a mobile unit that will be able to repair and/or replace tractor and truck tires on site including fields and road sides.

This statement is a bit longer than 50 words, but, perhaps more importantly, it succinctly lays out the nature of the business, including some of the short- and long-term goals. A concept statement might even be shorter:

> I want to start a commercial janitorial service that concentrates on providing janitorial services to offices owned by professionals, including accountants, lawyers, physicians, dentists, and other health care professionals and financial institutions.

> I want to open a pizza parlor that provides eat-in, carry-out, and delivery service on the corner of 5th and Walnut.

If you have a concept for a business, take time to write a concept statement now.

Will This Idea Really Work: Conducting a Feasibility Study

Once you have an idea about a business or businesses that you would like to start, you need to conduct a feasibility study. I suggest you use a force-field analysis of the problem of starting a business. This process begins with your concept paper, which lays out your goals: *I want to start an xyz business in this community.* Once your goals are stated, you begin by identifying all the driving and restraining forces related to your goal. Driving forces are those things that are moving you toward starting a business at this time, such as retirement, needing to make more money, fulfilling a life-long dream. Restraining forces are barriers to your success.

A list of restraining and driving forces might appear as follows:

Rocks in the road

1. I do not have a thorough knowledge of the competition that I must face.

2. I am unsure about the potential market for my product.

3. I will need additional money to start and operate the business.

4. I have very little experience starting and managing small businesses.

Motivators

1. I am totally committed to the idea and to starting a small business.

2. I can risk $15,000 of my own money to start the business.

3. I am very good with meeting and managing people. I can be persuasive.

Once you have made a list of forces that are barriers to starting your own business, then you begin to methodically eliminate them.

It's me or them, and I know who I am: Identify the competition

My plan for identifying the competition is as follows:

1. I will begin by making a list of all of the businesses that will compete with me if I begin XYZ by consulting the Chamber of Commerce's directory of local business and the yellow pages of the telephone book.

2. I will systematically compare the advantages and disadvantages (cost, quality, availability, flexibility) of the product or service that I intend to market with those of my prospective competitors.

3. I will try to determine the intangibles that give me an advantage (e.g., being able to personalize service) or are a disadvantage (name recognition by competitors) in the marketplace.

You will need to systematically attack each barrier to the establishment of your business if you are to be successful. You also may need to strengthen the driving or motivating forces by working on them systematically. For example, no one can deny that being good with people as well as being persuasive are important assets when starting a business. However, if you are going to be involved in persuading bankers or others to support your enterprise, you may want to hone your assets by reading books or taking courses that focus on motivating/persuading others, thus making an asset a more powerful force in your quest to start a business.

Write down the restraining and driving forces that may influence you as you start your own business.

Is Anyone Really Out There?: Sizing Up the Market

You've got a concept or, better, two or three ideas that are of interest to you. Perhaps you have decided to cater holiday meals for families or to start a handyman service that will provide repairs to homes that take a day or less to complete. The next step is to determine if there is a market for these products or services. A large corporation might do a careful market analysis by looking at the demographic characteristics of the populations, conducting a telephone survey of potential customers, conducting interviews or distributing samples in shopping malls, or simply starting a business on a trial basis to determine the outcome. While you won't be able to do all of these things, you can do them in a modified form.

You will know them by their age, income, and buying habits: demographics

Begin by defining the geographic area to be served by your business. This establishes the boundaries of your business. Next, look at the census data to determine the number of people living in your geographic area as well as their ages, ethnic background, average income, number of households with two wage earners, number of people who own their own homes versus those renting, and number of single family households. These data, which are typically available in your public library, can give you important clues to the need for services such as in-home health care (for the elderly), babysitting and day-care services (for young families with children), ethnic foods and products (for ethnic groups), travel services (for middle- and upper-income groups), home repair and gardening services (for home owners with both spouses working), food catering services (for middle- and upper-income groups). You can also order the *Census of Business,* which contains information about wholesale, retail, and service businesses; the *Statistical Abstract of the United States;* and the *County and City Data Book* from the Bureau of the Census (Federal Office Buildings 2 & 3, Suitland, MD 20233.) The *Abstract* and *Data* books give you information about income, employment patterns, ethnic characteristics, housing, age, and other information crucial to determining the potential market for the business you plan to start.

Many people wish to start businesses that are not oriented to a single geographic area, such as a roadside restaurant or a discount clothing shop. Because the failure rate of small businesses is excessive, it is recommended that you explore franchise possibilities in order to reduce the risk. More about this later.

Am I Going to Be Better or Just Different?: Competition Analysis

You will also want to get a listing of the numbers and types of businesses in your geographic area, both to determine the nature of the competition and to identify potential customers. As suggested, look carefully at the competition to determine if (1) the potential market for your product is saturated, (2) if, even when there are large numbers of competitors, there are segments of the market that are not saturated (ethnic groups, senior citizens, single parents), or (3) you can offer a better product or service at a higher cost and capture the "high-end" market, a better product or service at the same cost, or a product or service that is somewhat lower in quality at a lower price and capture the "low-end" market.

To Franchise or Not to Franchise: That Is the Question

Some people begin their business planning with the intention of purchasing a franchise, which is a proven way to reduce risks. The way it works is simple: you pay a franchise fee and usually a percentage of your income for services such as a complete market analysis; management training, including personnel recruitment and training strategies; nationwide advertising (and accompanying name recognition), and assistance with financing. For example, Mail Boxes Etc, a franchiser that establishes businesses that provide customers with mail boxes, mail forwarding service, package shipping, copying and faxing, and a variety of other services, currently charges a franchise fee of $19,500. For this fee, the franchiser offers the following services: two weeks of classroom training; focusing on establishing and operating your business; one week of in-store training; advertising and marketing materials; assistance with locating the business and lease negotiation; the opportunity to lease equipment; and on-going consultation regarding the operation of the business as well as ways to increase its profitability. The franchiser estimates that the total capital requirements for starting a business of this type is $45,000 to $70,000. Each year, *Entrepreneur Magazine* publishes a list of the leading franchisers and their minimum start-up costs. The 1992 list follows:

Franchiser	Prod/Serv	Minimum Start-Up Cost
McDonald's	fast food	$ 547,000
Subway	fast food	$ 44,000
Dunkin Donuts	fast food	$ 160,000
Jani-King	cleaning	$ 7,500
Baskin-Robbins	ice cream	$ 134,000
Service Master	cleaning	$ 16,800
Chem-Dry	cleaning	$ 9,950

Hardee's	fast food	$ 714,900
Arby's	fast food	$ 550,000
Domino's Pizza	fast food	$ 83,000
Dairy Queen	ice cream	$ 405,000
Choice Hotels	hotels	$1,510,000
Coverall America	cleaning	$ 3,600
Jazzercise	fitness	$ 2,325
Midas	auto repair	$ 192,000
Mail Boxes Etc	shipping	$ 54,000
7-Eleven	con. store	$ 12,500
H & R Block	income tax	$ 5,600
Coldwell Banker	real estate	$ 28,000
Blockbuster	video rental	$ 385,000
Budget Rent A Car	auto rental	$ 165,000
KFC	fast food	$ 80,000
Merle Norman	cosmetics	$ 3,300
Re/Max	real estate	$ 12,800

The prospective small business owner must decide whether the costs associated with a franchise can be justified in terms of the support provided and the risk reduction that accrues. However, it is probably a good idea to become familiar with the franchises that are available in the area in which you expect to start a business, because they are likely to be your competitors in the future. The booklet *Facts on Selecting a Franchise,* published by the Council of Better Business Bureaus in Arlington, Virginia, can be a useful guide in this process. So can *Evaluating Franchise Opportunities,* published by the U.S. Small Business Administration. If you decide to purchase a franchise, this latter publication offers the following guidelines for choosing the best franchise for you.

1. Find out how long the franchiser has been offering franchises, how many it has offered, and if any of them are in your geographic area.

2. Is the franchiser interested in your credentials, or does it seem interested in rushing to contract signing?

3. Determine the financial condition of the franchiser. According to the Federal Trade Commission, the franchiser must provide you with a full financial disclosure package 10 days prior to the signing of contracts.

4. Determine who owns the franchise. Have they ever been involved in fraud or other unlawful activities? Do they have expertise in the business that is being franchised?

5. Determine if earnings claims are accurate by talking to other franchisees. Will you earn a good return on the money you invest?

6. Identify the components of the franchise package. Are licensing fees, building costs, land costs, equipment, training initial inventory, promotional fees, and use of operating manuals covered?

7. Identify the continuing costs, such as royalties, training, advertising fees, insurance, and interest on money loaned by the franchiser.

Once you answer the foregoing questions, you are ready to select a franchise.

Lawyer Needed: Selecting a Legal Structure

Essentially you have three options: sole proprietorship, partnership, or incorporation. Of these, the sole proprietorship offers the advantage of simplicity since you need no assistance from an attorney to begin. Taxes are relatively straightforward as well since no separate forms have to be filed, although Schedule C must be appended to your individual income tax form. My wife and I have operated a business of this type for several years, and the only drawback seems to be that legally you and your business are the same. If you incur debts, your property, including your house, can be claimed by your creditors in lieu of the debt. You also face the same problems if an employee or customer files and wins a liability suit against you. One way to protect against this possibility is to have a large amount of liability insurance, but this can be quite costly.

The advantages and disadvantages of a partnership arrangement are essentially the same as those of the sole proprietorship, except it provides you with the opportunity to involve others in the establishment of the business. However, partnership agreements need to be carefully drawn, and thus an attorney should be involved. The business landscape is littered with failed businesses and lawsuits that grew out of informal partnership agreements. Partnership agreements specify extent of ownership; decision-making procedures and prerogatives of partners; a buy-out clause that specifies how partners may dispose of, and in some instances assume, the portion of the business owned by another partner; death benefits; and a variety of other variables.

Many small business owners will elect to incorporate because the business becomes the "whole enterprise," and thus their personal assets are usually protected from seizure by creditors and persons who win liability judgments against the business. Incorporation also allows the owners to issue stock both as an incentive to employees and as a way to capitalize the business. Stock issues are subject to state and national guidelines and typically require legal consultation. Increased legal fees and accounting fees are two of the drawbacks of incorporation, and there is the possibility of higher taxes, depending upon the type of corporation established. Tax laws designed to promote the establishment of small businesses now provide income tax breaks to corporations with limited numbers of shareholders.

In the final analysis, the question of the best legal structure can be answered only by consulting an attorney about your particular circumstances. When you select a lawyer, make sure that he or she has expertise in the area of small businesses.

The Matter of Money: Financing the Business

No question is more important to the prospective small business owner than, "How will I finance my business?" If you select a business that has a relatively low start-up cost, the typical answer will be that you will finance the start-up yourself. If the start-up costs are high, you will have to seek money from banks or other lenders. Whether you plan to start the business yourself or to seek money from outside sources, you need to begin by making several financial estimates.

You may wish to begin the process of estimating your start-up costs by determining your costs for equipment, furnishings, and rent or renovation costs.

Start-Up Costs

_____ Typewriters

_____ Computer

_____ Software

_____ Printer/label printer

_____ Fax machine

_____ Copy machine

_____ Telephones/answering machines

_____ File cabinets/desks/chairs/other office equipment

_____ Specialized equipment specific to this business

_____ Rent/remodeling

_____ Utility deposits

_____ Licenses or permits

_____ Liability/fire/theft/other insurance costs

_____ Initial advertising costs

_____ Deposits on inventory

_____ Legal/accounting/consulting fees

_____ Miscellaneous supplies and equipment

_____ Starting cash to pay expenses before sales begin

_____ Total start-up costs

The total start-up costs represent the amount of money you will need to open the doors and function for one month. After that point, you need another type of estimate that includes cash-in, that is, the cash your business receives from sales and other sources, and cash-out, which is the expense that you must pay each month. Cash-out includes salaries and fringe benefits, including Social Security taxes and workers' compensation insurance (in some instances), utilities, supplies, rent, and other costs such as payments on loans.

Your cash flow is the difference between the two. A positive cash flow means that cash-in exceeds cash-out. However, most people who begin small businesses plan for a negative cash flow during the formative stages of the business, which means they expect to pay out more money than they receive. The amount of money that you will need from outside sources will be the amount of start-up costs plus the amount of money you will need to carry you through that period where you are either losing money or are not making enough money to make payments on money owed to creditors subtracted from the money you have available to invest in the business.

total available cash + cash-in

− start-up costs + cash-out

———————————————————

= money needed from outside resources

Deciding from where to borrow the money is a major concern. Banks, some state agencies, and some federal agencies make loans to people wishing to start small businesses. Regretfully, we are not all as fortunate as the founder of Mrs. Field's Cookies, who borrowed the money from her husband to launch her highly successful small business.

A Rose by Any Other Name Wouldn't Be a Rose: Naming the Business

If you look at the yellow pages of your telephone book, you may conclude that not much energy goes into selecting business names, although there are exceptions. It is equally clear that people who market franchises focus a great deal of attention on business names. Try to determine the businesses engaged in by of each of the following:

1. Women at Large _____

2. Dial-A-Tile _____

3. Stress Solutions _____

4. The Pet Pourri _____

Franchiser number 1 helps people establish businesses that provide exercise and image enhancement for older women. Number 2 deals in shop-at-home ceramic tile businesses, and number 3 licenses stress reduction centers. Number 4 is a North Carolina business that sells a complete line of pet supplies. The names of these businesses communicate their product or service.

Not being concerned about the name of your business may ultimately be a fatal error, for unless you decide to select one of the popular franchises, name recognition is essential to your success. Get your family involved. Consider involving a communication consultant or an advertising firm. Study the names of your competitors. Make sure the name of your business sticks in the minds of potential customers.

Reach Out and Sell To Someone: The Marketing Plan

Not long ago, I surveyed a number of people who had started small businesses and asked them, "What advice would you give others who wish to follow in your footsteps?" The advice most frequently offered was to be prepared to market your business. One individual suggested that during the first year of your business, you should be prepared to spend 50 percent of your time in marketing. This business owner also advised that no one should forget that the need for marketing continues long after the business is established—in fact, it is an on-going commitment for the life of the business.

In developing a market plan, several factors must be considered, but ultimately the most important consideration is reaching customers at the lowest possible cost. My wife and a colleague wished to start a small business that would offer classes to people who are afraid to fly. They contacted the advertising editor of a local advertiser, who advised them that for $1,000 they could purchase the entire front page of the advertiser, which they did. The advertisement resulted in no calls. A short time later, a small advertisement in the personal services column of a local newspaper with the second-largest circulation in the state of North Carolina resulted in 15 telephone inquiries and seven enrollments in the class. The cost of this advertisement was $60. Why were the results so different? Although the reason for differential response is not clear, it seems likely that people do not look for personal services in an advertiser that specializes in used cars, furniture, and cleaning and repair services. It also may have been the differences in the circulation of the two newspapers.

A friend who owns a small landscaping and yard care business advertises by attaching rather crude flyers that describe his services to mail boxes. He estimates that he will receive calls and jobs from 5 percent of the people who receive the flyers. He designs the flyers, duplicates them at a local copy center, and distributes them at key times such as early spring, in the fall when leaves drop, and at planting time. He admits that this is a rather crude approach to marketing, but, as he put it, "I'm as busy as I want to be."

Factors such as the image you are trying to project, where your competition advertises, cost, and the type of business will dictate the approach taken to advertising. However, there are some approaches to advertising that should not be overlooked, because they are relatively inexpensive. As soon as you decide what business you intend to start, have some business cards produced which can be printed for as little as $10 per thousand and begin to hand them out to friends and associates. In this way you begin to take advantage of the most effective form of advertising: word of mouth. When the business is ready to open, write a press release that describes you and your business and send it to the local newspapers. Many of them will print it at no cost. Post well-designed fliers on community bulletin boards in places like apartment buildings, government office buildings, and public auditoriums. These will need to be reposted from time to time because they are removed periodically, but this is an inexpensive way to advertise your business.

Ultimately you will have to mount an advertising campaign to market your business, and the possibilities are endless. Radio stations, newspapers, the classified advertisements in the yellow pages of telephone books, and other advertisers usually have sales people who can explain factors such as cost, circulation, and the market segment they reach. Since many small businesses are designed to provide goods and services to a particular clientele, the population reached by the advertiser is of primary importance. You may also wish to use direct mailing services such as ValPac, which typically mails discount coupons to potential customers as a means of introducing them to a product or service or to encourage the continued patronage of an existing business. You will want to avoid the mistake that my wife and her colleague made by advertising in the wrong vehicle, although you may not know which type of advertising is best without some trial and error. You will also want to prepare an advertising budget that lists the approaches to marketing that you intend to use along with the amount of money you intend to expend for each approach.

To Leave Home or Not:
Selecting a Site

Once it has been determined to begin a business, the decision of where to locate the business must be made. One obvious choice is to clean out a spare bedroom, establish an office, and use that as a base for your operation. Carl McDaniels, in *The Changing Workplace,* lists the major advantages of working at home as (1) eliminates commuting, thus reducing auto costs and perhaps insurance costs as well; (2) less lost time in activities, such as getting ready for and commuting to work, and thus the opportunity for increased productivity; (3) reduced wardrobe, parking, and meal costs; (4) may reduce the need for day-care; (5) increased time with family; and (6) depending upon the type of business you intend to start, may give you flexibility about where you live, since you are not tied to commuting to a location for work. I would add two additional advantages to working out of your home to McDaniels's list. First, you can dramatically reduce your operating costs if you do not have to rent commercial property. Second, some tax benefits may accrue if your business is in your home. However, a 1992 Supreme Court ruling makes it mandatory that your business be primarily conducted in your home before this deduction can be claimed. A tax attorney or accountant should be consulted to determine if the office you plan will qualify under the new Internal Revenue Service guidelines.

McDaniels also lists several disadvantages of working at home. These are (1) your business may take up space needed for family, (2) you may become a workaholic at a time when you are trying to cut back because the business is too accessible, (3) the likelihood of interruptions in your private life are increased; it is easy for customers to rationalize calling or dropping by on weekends or in the evening if your business is in your home, (4) the "close quarters" that result from having a business in the home may increase conflicts within your family, (5) isolation from co-workers may result in loneliness, and (6) may feel unprofessional because you are not in a professional setting. Perhaps a bigger problem than feeling isolated and unprofessional is that prospective customers may not view your business as favorably if it is located in your home. One of the problems that some people have when they start a business is deciding whether they are really in business. This is certainly the case if the business grows out of a hobby or if you have very limited financial objectives.

A number of factors will ultimately influence your choice of a site for your business. First on this list should be those variables that relate to profitability. Answering the following questions may help you think about these factors.

1. How will choice of site influence my costs and thus the amount I must choose to charge for my service or product? How will this impact my competitiveness?

2. What type of customers do I hope to attract, and what is the likely impact of various sites on these customers?

3. Where are my competitors located and what advantages and disadvantages will various types of sites provide in my competition with them?

4. Am I dependent upon drive-by or walk-in customers, and, if so, what site will maximize the likelihood that these customers will access my business?

5. What are my goals for one, three, and five years? Can I test the viability of my idea in a home-based business and then move it to another site later?

6. How will the choice of a site influence my ability to secure financing?

7. Does the location of my home provide customers with the access and parking they will need?

8. What are the actual costs of the alternative sites available to me, and how do these costs fit into my plans for financing the business? (Include in these computations the potential reduction in costs of day-care, commuting, and tax savings that result from each alternative.)

9. What type of image am I trying to create, and how will this be influenced by various sites?

10. Which facility allows for future expansion?

11. Where can I get the best quality fire and police protection?

12. Are my competitors nearby, and is this good or bad?

After the profitability of the business is considered, personal factors should be considered. For example:

1. What will the impact of the sites I am considering be on me and my family?

2. In which site would I be happiest working?

3. Can I refrain from conducting business at home and thus diminishing my quality of life?

Once these questions have been answered, the choice of a site may be more obvious. However, like most business decisions, the answer may not be obvious, and you will have to make a decision based upon incomplete information. If you still are not sure which is the best site for you, a small business consultant may be helpful in reaching a final decision.

Finally, it is obvious that certain types of businesses are more easily adapted to a home base than others. If you decide to work at home, you may wish to consider some of the following businesses.

Meeting planner—plans meetings and outings for businesses.

Seminar producer—identifies community needs and books seminars to meet those needs. Handles all arrangements, including booking the presenter, arranging for advertisement and ticket sales, and leasing space for the seminar.

Tutor—provides tutoring services to elementary or high school students.

Information detective—searches books, technical documents, and computerized data bases to collect information for companies about new products that are being developed by competitors and research that is being produced in other settings such as universities.

Caterer—provides foodstuffs of various types to businesses and individuals.

Security systems sales person—installs and services security systems.

Craftsmaker—produces and markets various types of crafts.

Bed-and-Breakfast operator—provides overnight lodging and meals.

Consultant—provides various types of consulting services, ranging from computer systems to landscaping.

Yard care worker—cleans, mows, rakes, trims, plants, and does other tasks related to lawn care and maintenance.

Cleaning service owner—does residential and commercial cleaning.

Putting It All Together: The Business Plan

If you require outside capital to start your small business, you will need to prepare a detailed business plan. Even if you intend to finance the business yourself, most experts recommend that you draft a detailed business plan because it requires you to focus on the vital processes involved in starting and operating your business. A business plan contains the following elements:

1. The name and location of the business.

2. A detailed description of the product or service that you intend to offer, including a comparative analysis of your product or service with others offered in your market. Explain why you expect to be successful. If you are dependent upon suppliers of materials or foodstuffs, specify the arrangements you have made with them to ensure that you will have the products needed to operate your business.

3. A description of your competition. Which competitors are nearby? How are they doing financially?

4. A description of your target customers. Do you have a unique market niche? How large is the market in terms of dollars? Is it expanding?

5. An analysis of the economic contingencies that may influence your business (influx of senior citizens; home ownership is increasing).

6. Your marketing strategy. How will you advertise your product or service? What other marketing strategies will you use?

7. A description of the management of your business. Who will be involved, and what is their background and expertise?

8. A complete financial statement, including the current assets and liabilities of the business, projected start-up costs and expenses, projected cash flow.

9. The legal structure of the business (e.g., sole proprietorship, partnership, corporation).

Some Case Histories

Brenda The case of Brenda is instructive. She knew that she wanted to open her own business, and after working as a secretary for 20 years, she left her job as a state employee and enrolled in an eight-week small business management program in the local community college. After completing the program, she took a job in a local restaurant as an assistant manager. She rose quickly to the position of manager and then began to explore the possibilities of opening her own restaurant. She decided that the easiest and surest route to her goal was a franchise. Because she had training and experience, she was accepted as a franchisee. The franchise owners helped her prepare a business plan and negotiate for financial backing. Within three years of her decision to start her own business, she was operating two restaurants and considering opening a third.

Brenda had a goal and was able to translate it into action. Many potential business owners have ideas, sometimes dozens of them, but they cannot bridge the gap between concept and implementation.

Rick Rick never liked his job but held onto it for security because he had three children and all of the obligations that accompany a family of that size. As soon as his children finished college, he began to look into business opportunities. His goals were to identify a job that would have the potential of earning $100,000 annually, take him out of sales, and allow him more control over his time. He also wanted to minimize the amount of capital he invested since his family obligations had limited his savings. He purchased a territory containing 250,000 homes from a direct mail advertising franchiser, remodeled a bedroom, bought office equipment, a copier, and a facsimile machine and established his business.

Initially Rick solicited advertising from what he believed were more male-oriented businesses, and his wife solicited from female-oriented businesses. At this juncture, they are preparing to hire two direct commission sales persons, and both Rick and his wife will cut back on the amount of time they spend in sales. Eventually, both will withdraw from sales and spend their time managing the business. Rick admits that he hasn't reached the $100,000 mark yet but says he didn't expect to in two years. He still believes that the business has that potential. Perhaps more importantly, Rick has reached his goal of having more control over his time.

Tips for Getting Started

- Do a careful self-analysis of your motivation, skills, and risk taking. This is not a time to play games with yourself.

- Enroll in a course or workshop devoted to small business management at your local community college.

- Job shadow the manager of a small business. Walk a mile in his or her shoes for a day or two.

- Call the Small Business Administration for the name of the Small Business Development Center or Small Business Institutes nearest you. These centers, which are typically located in universities, provide free consultation to prospective entrepreneurs. They are typically staffed by business professors and advanced-level graduate students who can answer questions about everything from market research to the development of business plans.

- Get a part-time job in the type of business you expect to start.

- Read some of the current books on starting your own business such as *How to Really Start Your Own Business* by David E. Gumpert (Goldhirsh Group) or *101 Businesses to Start* by Sharon Kahn (Bantam Doubleday Publishing Group).

- If you are considering a franchise, read *Facts on Selecting a Franchise* by the Council of Better Business Bureaus of Arlington, Virginia. Also, order *Franchising World* and read it religiously. You can get your subscription started by calling 202-628-8000. You may also wish to contact the American Franchise Association, 2730 Wilshire Boulevard, Suite 400, Santa Monica, CA 90403. *Entrepreneur Magazine,* the *Wall Street Journal,* and other business publications regularly carry articles about franchises as well as other small business opportunities. You may wish to start reading some or all of these publications.

- If you have decided against a franchise and you are leaning toward a home-based business, read some of the following: *Starting and Operating a Home-Based Business* by D. R. Eyler (John Wiley & Sons) or *Starting and Managing a Business from Your Home* by L. Waymonn and published by the Small Business Administration in Washington, D.C. You may also wish to read the book by Kennedy and Arden, *Home Businesses under $5000.* This book is published by Sun Features of Cardiff, CA. You may also wish to subscribe to the newsletter *Home Business Line,* published by the American Home Business Association located in Darien, CT 06820, or to *Mind Your Own Business,* published by the National Association of Cottage Industries. The editors can be contacted by writing Box 14460, Chicago, IL 60614.

- Get the Small Business Administration's list of video tapes and booklets by ordering *The Small Business Directory* from SBA Publications, Box 30, Denver, CO 80201-0030.

- Call 1-800-827-5722, the Small Business Answer Desk, to get more information about SBA's programs and services.

Summary   Starting your own business is a big step and must be considered in light of the retirement life-style you have chosen. Once you have decided that you do want to begin a business, there are many resources that can be accessed, not the least of which is the Small Business Administration. However, the best advice to people who wish to start their own businesses may be to work in the type of business they wish to start for a few weeks. This experience will help them solidify their decision to start a business and will give them added credibility with lending institutions if financing is required.

Consulting For Fun and Profit

Did you know that worldwide consulting firms took in more than 28 billion dollars in 1992 and that the money paid for consulting is expected to increase rapidly?

The Consulting Revolution
Consulting is big business. The top 15 consulting firms in the United States employ nearly 90,000 consultants and take in over 11 billion dollars annually, according to the Associated Press. Additionally, there are thousands of small consulting firms, and the number grows daily. The total revenue generated by all consultants in this country

is estimated to exceed 15 billion dollars, a number that increases yearly.

What has brought about this consulting revolution? First, because of downsizing, many corporations have lost valuable expertise, expertise available only through consultants. One electrical engineer was hired as a consultant by the company that had just laid him off. The company saved the 30 percent of his salary it was paying in fringe benefits, and he was able to spend less time on the job—a win-win situation. Other corporations have found that, because of their restructuring efforts, not only is the expertise to solve problems lacking but so is the time. The result: consultants are hired to solve problems that would have been tackled internally prior to restructuring.

Restructuring is only one reason consulting businesses are booming. The increasing use of technology has created the need for consultants to teach businesses how to get the most bang for their bucks invested in expensive technology. In fact, in many instances, businesses that install expensive new technology have to be shown how to use it initially.

All businesses are interested in ways they can improve their bottom lines, and thus they demand consultants who can help them improve marketing, customer service, decision making, record keeping, inventory control, or any other aspect of the business. However, this is not to suggest that there is a shortage of consultants. In fact, consulting is one of the most intensely competitive businesses around. Prior to hanging out a shingle as a consultant, several factors need to be taken into consideration.

What do consultants sell? Consultants sell expertise. Are there areas where you can improve the product certain companies produce? Or do you know how to improve business processes? Companies produce two types of products: goods and services. Typically they function in a competitive environment, that is, other businesses also produce the same type of goods or services. Only about 15 percent of the businesses in the United States actually produce goods such as automobiles, steel, and appliances. However, in the last decade, these businesses have spent millions of dollars to hire consultants that would improve their products, primarily because of competition from Japan and Europe. This consulting help has focused on everything from the use of plastics in the manufacture of automobiles to the formation of work teams that will reduce the number of problems resulting from the manufacturing process. Dry cleaners, restaurants, and mechanics provide services. Service-producing businesses are also concerned about quality, the quality of the service they produce. Just as importantly, service-producing businesses must concern themselves with the manner in which they interact with their customers as they provide the service. These businesses spend millions of dollars on consulting to improve customer relationships.

Both goods- and service-producing businesses must be concerned about marketing and sales; business processes, such as accounting and record keeping; management, including decision making and leadership; planning, including the establishment of long- and short-term plans; personnel relationships, including hiring and downsizing; acquisitions and mergers; and a host of other issues. If you have, or can develop, expertise in one or more of these areas, you may have the right stuff to become a consultant. The following is a list of areas that have been hot topics in the consulting area.

Stress management

Quality control

Excellence audits

Building collaborative work teams

Self-directed work teams

Self-directed workers

Leadership skills for supervisors

Improving managers' coaching skills

Creative problem solving

The Abilene Paradox (false consensus in decision making)

Performance management/feedback

Creating/recreating corporate culture

Empowering employees/managers

Defining organizational values

Value-added approaches to managing organizational resources

Work and organizational group dynamics

Improving the effectivenesss of meetings

Conflict resolution

Negotiation

Managerial/leadership styles

Situational leadership

Strategic planning

Multicultural relationships in the workplace

What is my credibility?

Having expertise is not enough. In order to get hired, consultants must have credibility, which is based either on successful experience, educational background, or both. One $10,000-per-day consultant to major oil companies has a bachelor's and master's degree in petroleum engineering and 20 years of experience in various facets of the petroleum industry, including oil field acquisitions. Most consultants are not paid $10,000 per day. The average fee is between $600 and $1000 per day, but to command any consulting fee, you will need credentials.

A common credential held by business consultants is the MBA, master's degree in business administration. Many young people with MBAs join consulting firms at salaries ranging from $30,000 to $90,000 per year, based on the status of the institution where they got their degrees, their grades, and their experiences. Other consultants have degrees in organizational psychology, personnel relationships, industrial relations, communications, and a host of others. Some technical consultants hold degrees in engineering, computer science, and chemistry. Often businesses hire consultants who are specialists in their field such as textiles, forestry management, horticulture, floriculture, or advertising. If you are not going to become a consultant based upon your success in business, a degree is essential for credibility.

In many instances, the best credential for a consultant is past success. If you can show that you have successfully solved thorny business problems, you have the basis for establishing a consulting business.

Becoming A Consultant:
Two Tracks

Figure 5.1 shows the top 15 consulting firms in the United States. As noted, they employ nearly 90,000 consultants. The yellow pages of your telephone book will help you identify which of these companies are located in your area. The "consultants/consulting" listing will also help you identify other types of consulting opportunities.

FIGURE 5.1

Top 15 U.S. Consulting Firms

1. Anderson Consulting
2. McKinsey & Co.
3. Coopers & Lybrand
4. Ernst & Young
5. Mercer Consulting
6. Peat Marwick
7. Deloitte & Touche
8. Price Waterhouse
9. Towers Perrin
10. Booz-Allen Hamilton
11. CSC Consulting Group
12. Gemini Consulting
13. Wyatt Co.
14. Hewiit Associates
15. American Management Associates

Source: Ferrell Kramer, "Path to a Nation of Consultants," the Associated Press, 1993.

A local telephone book contains listings for the following types of consultants listed in figure 5.2.

FIGURE 5.2

Specialized Consulting Firms

1. Building construction consultants
2. Business consultants
3. Data systems consultants
4. Educational consultants
5. Engineering consultants
6. Executive search consultants
7. Financial consultants
8. Hospital consultants
9. Management Consultants
10. Marketing consultants
11. Personnel consultants
12. Real estate consultants
13. Safety consultants
14. Wedding consultants
15. Insurance consultants
16. Investment consultants
17. Computer systems designers and consultants

Each of the firms listed in figures 5.1 and 5.2 offer many services. One of the major firms, Coopers & Lybrand, offers the consulting services in the following areas:

Auditing

Accounting

Tax planning

Tax compliance

Personal financial planning (for executives)

Outsourcing

Risk management

Organizational effectiveness

Employee communication

Technology applications

Record keeping

Retirement and health benefits

Actuarial consulting

Internal audit

Performance appraisal

Human resources services

Compensation plans

Data management

These and other services are offered by many firms. The consulting firms listed in figures 5.1 and 5.2 are but a few of the opportunities available. If you have a skill, you can probably find a way of utilizing it in an existing consulting firm.

The Life-Style of the Consultant

The idea of being a consultant appeals to many because of the stereotype they hold of the position. Consultants are often viewed as world travelers rushing here and there to save businesses from ruin for large fees. In fact, many consultants are paid handsome fees, and some do jet to exotic places and work with exciting projects. However, most consultants apply the expertise they have to solving practical problems in rather mundane settings. Helping a hospital set up a new record-keeping system is not particularly exciting. Neither is helping a business get higher productivity out of the new technology it just purchased. Consulting jobs rarely happen in romantic locations, either.

Consultants find that their life is sometimes feast, sometimes famine. They are always marketing themselves and their services to avoid famine. In fact, some consultants told me recently that new consultants should expect to spend 100 percent of their initial work load marketing and that the marketing end of the job will probably never go below 40 to 50 percent of their time. Unfortunately, no matter how much time you spend marketing, the work load will be uneven in almost all cases, and so will the income. For people who have been accustomed to a regular income, the ambiguity about salary can be quite upsetting.

The retiree who is considering consultation as an easy way to ease out of retirement and expects to make money at it may end up being disillusioned. Unless you can take your job with you, like the electrical engineer, starting a consulting career is very hard work, often requiring long days, meeting strict deadlines for consulting proposals and reports, and arduous travel schedules. The good news for successful consultants is that they can earn a solid income. The bad news is that they will become very familiar with airline food and hotel accommodations.

Starting Your Own Consulting Firm

In the preceding chapter, the process of establishing your own business was discussed in some detail. Many of the same problems discussed in that chapter also face the would-be consultant. However, some of the unique aspects of establishing a consulting firm will be discussed here. Let me begin by telling you my own consulting story. Since I first became a professor, I have served as a consultant, and over the past 25 years, I have consulted with public schools; community colleges; universities; local, state, and federal government agencies; law firms; large and small businesses; and community mental health agencies. About 10 years ago, I decided that my consulting was interfering with my role as a university professor, and I ended all of my consulting relationships except one. What I discovered later when I decided to reenter the consulting arena is that I didn't really understand how I had generated my original consulting practice. It seemed to have materialized out of thin air. It hadn't. It had developed because I was a highly visible professional who appeared to have some expertise that would be useful to various groups. The more visible I became and the more expertise I seemed to possess, the more consulting business I received. Your problem is to make yourself visible and to make people aware of your expertise.

Starting with your old employer

The first place to look for a consulting job is where you last worked. You have visibility there because you know the people. You should also be familiar with the products and the business processes. If you have concrete ideas about how to remedy problems that you observed when you worked there, put a proposal together and go for it. The worst thing that can happen to you is that you will get turned down, but it is an opportunity to practice making a presentation in a relatively safe environment.

Ask your friends

Sit down and make a list of your friends and acquaintances that might need the service you intend to provide. Approach them on a business-like basis, that is, don't expect to be hired as a consultant because you are friends. Make it very clear that you expect to be hired on the basis of merit. But you would be very surprised how much personal relationships play in the hiring of consultants.

Increasing visibility in new areas

There are many ways that you can increase your visibility, some of which are obvious and some not so obvious. Strategically placed announcements of the opening of a practice can get initial attention but will probably not generate much business. Listings in the yellow pages of the telephone book and advertisements in local newspapers, business publications, and trade magazines may generate some business but are expensive.

One of the most effective ways to gain visibility is through personal contacts. Joining service organizations that have potential clients as members is always a good strategy. Even better, give speeches to organizations that have potential clients as members. Volunteering for organizations like the chamber of commerce can also bring you into contact with potential clients in the business world.

The time-honored person-to-person approach, the business lunch, is another effective approach to gaining consulting clients. For this to be effective, you must first identify the person who will hire consultants with your expertise. Then make a telephone contact, introduce yourself and the consulting service you are providing, and invite the person to lunch as your guest. Select a restaurant for the luncheon that is frequented by people like the potential client, but make sure that it provides an atmosphere that is conducive to conversation. Don't open the luncheon with business. Start by getting to know your new acquaintance, and take this opportunity to get to know more about her or his concerns. Then make a brief presentation of your service, provide a written description of the service so it can be reviewed later, and leave a business card with information about where you are located and how you can be contacted. Follow up the luncheon in a week or two if the prospective client seems at all interested.

Conducting workshops is not only a means of making money, but it can help you attract consulting clients as well. Consultants hold workshops on everything from negotiations with employees to conducting more effective staff meetings. If you do hold a workshop, make very certain that it has an aura of class. Select a first-class hotel or conference center for the meeting. Make sure that materials are tastefully done and are absolutely error free. Use well-designed audiovisual aids and make sure that you have a backup VCR, slide projector, or other piece of audiovisual equipment. "No glitches" is the rule. Dress to impress, and be sure your presentation is as flawless as you can make it. The workshop should be a metaphor for how well organized, knowledgeable, and impressive you can be.

Public speeches to civic clubs can gain you clients, but they are usually gratis. If you really have good platform skills, join a speakers' bureau and get into the business of after-dinner and motivational speeches. You may not be able to demand the $5000 or more fee of a Zig Ziglar, but with good skills, you can earn $500 or more for a single speech. Speeches also provide you with the opportunity to enhance your visibility.

Direct written solicitations are also effective ways to get clients. Generally, these go to presidents or CEOs of small companies and to the managers or directors in charge of the area where you hope to provide a service if the businesses or agencies are large. While some large consulting firms send out mass mailings, that is generally impossible for consultants just opening a business. My suggestion is to target the corporations or agencies that you hope to assist, do your homework to determine their positional needs, and then write letters to identify the type of consulting service you can perform.

If you write well, you may also wish to contribute articles to applied professional journals, develop a column in the local newspaper, or start a newsletter. Newsletters can be marketed and provide an additional source of income in addition to adding to your visibility.

Expertise   Consultants need a variety of skills if they are to be successful. As noted, they need something to sell, whether it be how to improve a product or a process. However, in order to be successful, consultants must also have good interpersonal skills, public speaking skills, and writing skills. Think about your skills as you complete the following checklist.

Consulting Skills

PERSONAL SKILLS

YES   NO   1.   I am persuasive. I have the ability to make others see my point of view.

YES   NO   2.   I persevere. When I am knocked down, I keep coming back for more.

YES   NO   3.   I am friendly. People relate to me easily.

YES   NO   4.   I am a good listener.

YES   NO   5.   I am assertive if I need to be.

YES   NO   6.   I am decisive.

YES   NO   7.   I am a good judge of character. I can usually tell how others will respond.

YES   NO   8.   I can communicate clearly on a one-to-one basis.

YES   NO   9.   I have a high energy level.

YES   NO 10.   I can produce under pressure.

_____ **TOTAL YES RESPONSES**

FUNCTIONAL SKILLS

YES   NO   1.   I have good technical writing skills.

YES   NO   2.   I can write succinct business proposals.

YES   NO   3.   I can write clear reports.

YES   NO   4.   I can make effective presentations to small and large groups.

YES   NO   5.   I can either produce or have resources that can produce high-quality handouts and materials.

YES   NO   6.   I can either produce or have resources that can produce high-quality audiovisual aids to support presentations.

YES   NO   7.   I have at least one marketable skill.

YES   NO   8.   I can quickly determine if an organization can benefit from what I have to offer and explain in clear terms what the benefits of using my services might be.

YES   NO   9.   I have the skills needed to organize a consulting business.

YES   NO 10.   I can identify and use other people who can support me if necessary.

_____ **TOTAL YES RESPONSES**

If you have fewer than seven "yes" responses in either the area of personal or functional skills, you need to seriously consider whether establishing a consulting business is for you. A low number of "yes" responses does not necessarily mean that you will not be a successful consultant, particularly if you have a skill that is in demand. It may mean that the best route to consulting as an occupation is through an established firm, however.

The Office
The decision regarding the location of your consulting office is an important one. As you may recall from chapter 4, there are many factors that should be considered when locating a business. These same general principles apply when considering the location of your consulting office with one exception: if you expect to consult with business from the outset and Fortune 500 companies are among your target clients, don't list 300 Spruce Street as your address. Rent an office in the most prestigious location your cash flow will allow. The appearance of success is an important credential in this area. You need to always be mindful that you are competing for business with Big Six accounting firms unless you have a highly specialized business that they or the other giants of the consulting world have not discovered.

The location and type of office may not be as important if you are consulting with small businesses, governmental agencies, and the like. In fact, because they are unable to pay the large fees that major businesses can, keeping down your overhead is a major concern because your income is likely to be smaller.

Sources of Income

Fees
The fees you charge your clients will be the major source of income in most consulting businesses, and thus it is important that you consider your fee structure at the outset. In establishing your fee, it is important to consider your overhead first. What is the total cost of rent, personnel, telephone, utilities, office supplies, and equipment? If you are operating out of an office in your home and your "personnel" consists of an answering machine and your equipment inventory is a fax machine and a word processor, then your overhead is minimal, but you still want to recover the costs in addition to receiving a fee for your services.

What should the fee be? There are two aspects to the answer to this question. One aspect has to do with what a particular client is ready to pay. The other is the amount of money that you are willing to accept to consult. If the client is willing to meet your minimum, a consulting contract may result. Major consulting firms establish hourly rates ranging from $75 to over $300 per hour for consulting services, but these are not their minimums. In fact, they rarely receive these rates, because every consulting job is negotiated with the client. If the client has a set budget for a job and if you will not serve as consultant for the established rate, another consultant will be sought. In other instances, clients will solicit bids from various consultants and the chore will be to be competitive while still making money, that is, making at least your minimum. Establish your minimum rate by figuring your overhead and the least amount of money that will be needed to employ you. Then, try to get an estimate of what the market will bear. That becomes your desired rate.

Other sources of income

Two potential sources of income that have already been mentioned are conducting workshops and giving speeches. However, an important source of income for many consultants lies in the products they produce. Some consultants market manuals they develop to improve performance appraisal if consulting contracts do not preclude the use of developed material, as they sometimes do. However, even if you are forbidden to publish material directly, you can develop materials based upon your consulting experiences. Consultants who specialize in employee motivation may be able to develop motivational posters that could be marketed to a wide variety of businesses. Financial consultants can develop brief guides to financial planning, investing, purchasing life insurance, estate planning, or purchasing stocks and bonds. Books on improving customer service, being a more effective sales person, and self-analysis are all potential by-products of consulting efforts.

Summary

Consulting is a potentially lucrative job for those retired workers who have a saleable skill and the companion skills needed for success in this competitive field. The attractive part of consulting for many is the possibility of using the skills they have developed over a lifetime and making money doing it. It is easy to underestimate the difficulty of getting into a business that is dominated by a number of giant consulting firms. However, as the yellow pages listings will attest, many individuals and small groups are involved in this multifaceted enterprise.

Resources For The Consultant

The following resources are available from University Associates, 8517 Production Avenue, San Diego, CA 92121-2280.

Block, P. *Flawless Consulting: A Guide To Getting Your Expertise Used.*

Lippitt, G., and R. Lippit, *The Consulting Process in Action* (2d ed.).

Schrello, D.M. *The Complete Marketing Handbook for Consultants.*

Shenson, H.L. *The Contract and Fee-setting Guide for Consultants and Professionals.*

University Associates and Blanchard Training and Development (127 State Place, Escondido, CA 92029) publish a wide variety of material that can be useful in management consulting.

The Job Hunt: Locating Retirement Jobs

Did you know that the most effective means of getting jobs in today's labor market is through networking?

Some self-help career books would lead you to believe that locating jobs is a simple process. It may be, depending on the type of job you seek. Part-time jobs in fast food restaurants, as cashiers in supermarkets and restaurants, and as sales clerks in retail outlets are relatively easy to locate and acquire. The demand is high, the turnover great, and the ads in store windows and elsewhere are ever present. If you are looking for a job that requires little investment of time and energy and consequently may return little in the way of personal satisfaction and monetary rewards, your task is easy. If, on the other hand, you are seeking a more challenging job, one for which there will be considerable competition, the task is difficult and requires considerable psychological preparation, some well-developed "tools," and no small amount of skill. This chapter will deal with sources of information about jobs and will delve into some general strategies for the job hunter. The chapter that follows will address the tools and skills the job hunter needs to follow up on leads that are identified in the job search.

Psychological Preparation for the Hunt

Have several options

Once you have determined the types of jobs that interest you, carefully consider the task ahead. First, if you have only one career objective, you run the risk of failure. Recently I received a letter from a friend who has retired from teaching school and wishes to become a flight attendant. Her interests in this career were stimulated when she shared with me a girlhood dream of "flying the friendly skies." I encouraged her to pursue the fantasy that she still harbored since she could retire with a full pension from her teaching job. Within a few months of giving that advice, most major airlines placed a moratorium on hiring flight attendants as they began the downsizing process. They will hire again in the near future, but she is increasingly frustrated because she cannot secure the job she wants immediately. If she perseveres, she has the right stuff to be a great flight attendant, and the job will allow her the time off she needs to enjoy the flight benefits that are far more important to her than the salary. My advice to her is to be patient. She has waited 30 years. A few more months of waiting should be bearable.

It is rare when an entire industry places a moratorium on hiring, but the ebb and flow in the hiring process in today's labor market can be quite unpredictable. Therefore, my first rule for the retired job hunter is have several options. Pursuing a single alternative may leave you as frustrated as my would-be flight attendant friend. A successful lawyer who has tired of defending criminals and wants to retire and take up a second career articulated this idea as follows: "I'm pursuing four different options (teaching law; managing a music company; changing specialties from criminal to corporate law; or mentoring new lawyers). One of them is bound to pay off." He is probably right. My only additional suggestion is that these options should be prioritized. What is his first choice, second choice, and so forth?

Be ready for bad news

Rule 2 of the job hunt process is prepare yourself psychologically for bad news. Almost every modern job seeker has a few tales of woe to tell about the process. I recently received a letter from a would-be career changer who had considerable experience and training in the area of health care administration. He had been seeking a job for six months and was wondering if he should set his sights lower (he had been seeking a high-level position) or change his objectives altogether. His financial position, his willingness to accept and be satisfied in a lower-level job, and his willingness to retrain all become factors in whether to lower his aspirations or change his goals. I advised him to broaden the geographic base of his job hunt. When job searchers are looking for a high-level management position, they should consider an entire region instead of confining themselves to a single state. However, both he and my would-be flight attendant friend are increasingly frustrated with the doors being slammed in their faces and are wondering what to do next. It is very easy to become discouraged and drop out of the search altogether under these circumstances unless you understand that in today's labor market the job search can be a difficult process.

Set realistic goals.   Three things can help you prepare for bad news. The first of these is setting realistic goals. The title of a recent self-help book suggests that anyone can land an exciting new career in 30 days or less. This is ridiculous. The average job hunter in this country takes from three to six months to secure employment unless he or she starts his or her own business or consulting firm. There is no reliable source of information about how many rejections these people receive before getting a new job, but a dozen or more would probably be a conservative estimate, and some job hunters receive hundreds of rejection notices.

Build a support network.   The second way that you can prepare yourself for the frustration that may accompany searching for a job is to build a support network. Social support is a tried and true method of helping people deal with stressors. Whom should you include? Obviously your family members, friends, and other job hunters. There will be more about this last group later, but we know that commiseration with people who are experiencing the same frustration and problems is an effective way to avoid the burnout that can occur. You will need sympathetic ears, not people who tell you, "You've worked enough. Enjoy your retirement years."

Have fun. The third strategy for dealing with frustration is to continue to engage in leisure and family activities. Job hunting must be treated like a job, but not an all-consuming one. Take time away from the process to have fun. It is entirely irrational to entertain the following thoughts:

- I must find the perfect job; otherwise, my life will be ruined.

- If people reject me, there is something wrong with me.

- The world is unfair; otherwise, I would be offered a job.

The Overall Strategy

Before you begin the job hunt, lay out an overall strategy. Will it be a local, state, regional, or national search? Will it focus on a single option or multiple options? Is there a timeline for getting the job? Who will serve as my support network? How much time, energy, and money am I willing to expend to acquire a job? The typical recommendation in terms of time is that if you are looking for a full-time job, spend 40 hours per week. This number may be reduced if you are looking for a part-time job, but the point is to be successful, you need to spend significant amounts of time on the job hunt. Similarly, the job hunt is not without costs. Business cards, resumes, and letterhead stationery are all necessary tools in the job hunt, and they all cost money. Depending on the geographic area you are covering, long distance telephone calls and fax charges can be significant. Accessing electronic data bases, mileage and car expenses, registration with private job placement firms, and purchasing clothing for interviews can all add to the cost of the job hunt. Computers, fax machines, modems, and laser printers are also tremendous assets for the job hunter, but they are also very expensive. Fortunately, national copying services such as Kinko's and Copytron make these machines available at relatively low costs, but visiting these centers will add significantly to the amount of time you spend on your job search. The point here is simple: before you begin your job search, you need to carefully assess your commitment to the process and decide whether you are willing to spend the time and money needed to be successful.

Locating Retirement Job Openings

There are several major approaches to locating job openings. The objective of this portion of the job search is to identify jobs that are of interest and for which you qualify. Job hunters most often consult newspaper advertisements that list job openings, according to a national survey I co-designed that was administered by the Gallup organization. Other sources of information about job openings include electronic databases; college placement offices (yes, this service is still open to you, although there may be a fee!); private and public employment agencies; newsletters of professional organizations; job postings within organizations; and other people, including other job seekers. It is this last group that I will discuss first.

The Job Search with a Thousand Eyes

Networking is a process by which a large number of people are made aware of your career aspirations. In the Gallup survey, 25 percent of the workers responding indicated that they used no sources of information about jobs. That is obviously not true. What is true is that many of the job openings that exist are not widely advertised, that is, they are not listed in employment offices or advertised in the newspaper, which offer the most extensive types of job listing. The result is that people hear about them through informal channels, often in a haphazard manner. At one time, the chief source of information about available jobs was other family members. Today, family members are still important sources of information, but the skilled job hunter casts a wider net to catch the right job.

If you are looking for a job, you need to have at least 500 other people helping you identify job openings. In order to accomplish this, you need a modicum of assertiveness, business cards, and a resume. The development of resumes will be discussed in chapter 7. However, an attractive, well-designed business card is essential to your networking efforts. This card should contain your name, followed by your highest degree earned, address, and telephone number. Print shops and businesses like Office Depot can help you design an eye-catching card. Consult the yellow pages of your telephone directory under "business cards" or "printers" for local resources.

How should you proceed to network? Figure 6.1 illustrates a networking map. First, make a list of friends, family members, club members, and former business associates who might be of assistance in locating the type of job you are seeking. Make a list of their names, addresses, and telephone numbers, preferably on computer, so that they can be recalled easily. Call or personally contact each of these people, making a note of the date they are contacted. This is the first tier of your network. During the contact, explain the type of job you are seeking and either hand them your resume and business card or send it to them with a thank-you letter reiterating the reason for the call and telling them how much you appreciate their assistance. Importantly, ask every person you contact if he or she can give you the name of a person or persons who might be able to help you find the type of job you want. Get the names, addresses, and telephone numbers of those people. Importantly, ask your friend or associate if he or she minds if you use his or her name when making the contact. Also ask your first tier of contacts if they would mind if you contact them again in a month or so to see if they have gotten any job leads that might be of interest. This places the responsibility for follow-up squarely on your shoulders. Of course, you should invite this primary tier of contacts to call you directly if they get any promising leads.

The second tier of people in your network should be contacted in the same manner as the first. These contacts will be a bit trickier, because typically you will not have met them. Having been referred by a mutual acquaintance will help break the ice in many instances, and this is the reason for using the names of the people in your primary tier when making the contacts. Once you have explained the purpose for your call—getting a job—and asking them if they can provide assistance in this area, you once again pop the question: "Do you know anyone who might either help me find the type of job of interest to me or be interested in employing me?" Your second tier leads to a third tier, which leads to a fourth tier, and so on.

Your initial approach to networking begins with friends and acquaintances. Your second foray is done on a deliberate but more random basis. Whenever you play golf, attend social gatherings or service club meetings, or go to church, you should carry a handful of business cards. Tell the people you meet in these settings about your career objective, give them a business card, and ask the same question, "Do you know anyone who might be interested in employing someone like me?"

Your third approach to networking may involve attending support groups for people seeking employment. These groups are regularly listed in public service announcements and in the employment section of the want ads, but they are more likely to appear in the Sunday paper than the weekly editions. Call your local newspaper to get specifics. Attend these groups with ready business cards and resumes. Many job seekers uncover jobs for which they are unqualified or in which they have no interest. They will gladly share that information with you. You should also be ready to share any information you have unearthed in your search.

Finally, your networking efforts should continue once you start to contact businesses about employment opportunities.

If the person you contact does not have the job you desire, perhaps he or she knows someone who does.

Following up

Follow-up calls and visits should begin within a month of the initial contact. In these follow-ups you do not want to make a pest of yourself, but perseverance is the most essential ingredient in the successful job hunt.

As noted, your computer can be of great assistance in organizing your networking contacts, and I suggest you organize them initially by tiers. You can also use a notebook or other hand-written record-keeping system, but the task gets quite laborious if you accomplish your objective of contacting 500 people. Regardless of whether you use a hand-written or computerized system, you should record the following information about each contact:

Name

Business/address

Telephone

Date contacted

Call back (yes/no/date)

Date resume sent/Thank-you sent

Leads provided

FIGURE 6.1

Networking Map

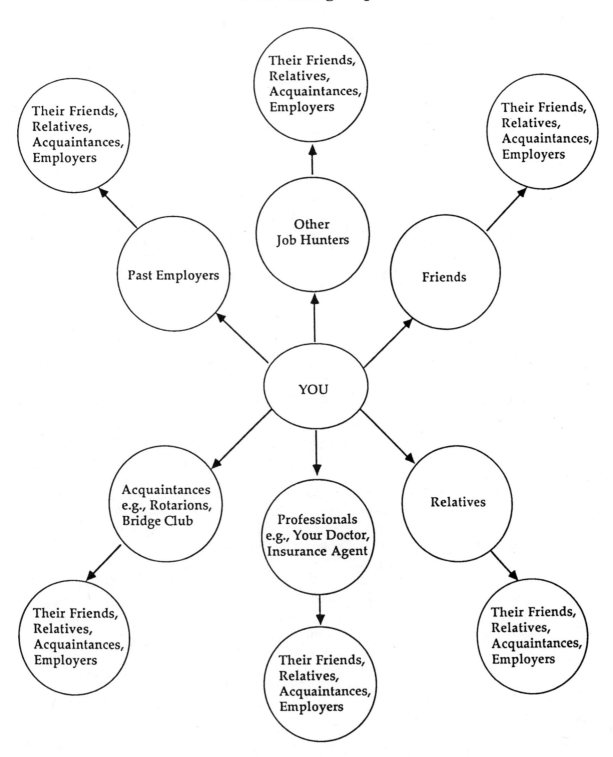

After the round of follow-up contacts, you may wish to eliminate some names because they do not seem to be very productive or because they are obviously not interested in assisting you. Importantly, send thank-you notes to those people who do help you. Americans have forgotten the fine art of saying thanks, so your gratitude will be appreciated, and you will be remembered. To simplify this task, a label-printing device and a program such as Label Writer II can be quite helpful, because you can enter the names in your tiers into an address book and print out professional-looking labels quite easily. Also, you can place a form letter on your computer and use it to send thank-you notes. There are even programs, such as Letterwriter for Job Seekers, which is available from Wintergreen Software, Inc. This software contains letters of inquiry, thank-you letters, and letters of application. These letters can be easily personalized by changing a few words or lines. An informal style thank-you note is quite acceptable, particularly if you know the person well. For persons that you do not know, a more formal style of writing is probably safer. A sample informal note follows.

Mr. Richard Hanks
1223 Ragsdale Road
Allentown, WV 25678

Dear Dick:

Thanks for taking a few minutes to discuss my re-careering plans and for the valuable leads you provided. I will be contacting them in the near future as I work toward my goal. Many people have told me that I should relax and enjoy my retirement, but I want to climb a few more hills, and I have the wherewithal to do it. I'm going to make someone a heck of a sales representative.

Enclosed is the resume I promised. Feel free to share it with anyone who might be interested. I would be glad to hear from you or anyone about a job that will allow me to use my skills.

Thanks again. I'll call you in a month.

Sincerely,
Jane Q. Job Hunter

Networking ends when you get the job you want, unless you are already seeking another job.

Cold Calls: Creating Your Own Job

I have a friend that never worries about job vacancies when her gad-about husband decides to take another job. Years ago she discovered the strategy of creating her own job, which means identifying opportunities that even the businesses or agencies who hire you have not recognized. In workplaces as dynamic as the current ones where decisions are based more on bottom-line concerns than good business practice in many instances, these opportunities abound.

In a sense, making cold calls is an extension of the networking process. Cold calls have traditionally been direct contacts with employers to determine if they either now have a vacancy that would be attractive to you or anticipate having one in the near future. These calls, which are often made by telephone but can be handled in person, are made without any definite indication that a job is available or that the employer is hiring. In the past, job hunters often made these calls to personnel managers, which was a mistake. It is important for you to know that this method, as it has been practiced in the past, is one of the least productive means of getting a job and has been one of the most disheartening. Why? Because job hunters made call after call to prospective employers and got the door slammed in their faces over and over again, sometimes in a very rude fashion. Many personnel officers and managers have taken steps to insulate themselves from people who are making cold calls asking for jobs. Typically they do this by having secretaries prescreen calls and eliminate job seekers. However, cold calls, if reconceptualized, can be turned into a productive job-hunting strategy.

If you are going to use cold calls to your advantage, you need to do your homework and get certain questions answered. Your objective in making a cold call should not be to determine if a job is available. It should be to create a job for yourself. First, you want to determine who in the company might hire you, given your particular set of skills. Personnel managers are rarely in charge of making hiring decisions. They may be instrumental in identifying candidates, conducting initial screening interviews, and verifying credentials, but the final decision about who will be hired typically rests with the manager for whom the employee will work.

Second, you want to identify the primary initiatives of the company and uncover the new, if any, directions that are about to be undertaken. One way to get this type of information is to access one or more of the many data bases that are currently available regarding businesses. Dun's Electronic Business Directory, Prodigy, and Standard and

Poor's On-Line Services are excellent sources of information about corporations and may provide the information you need to get started. Another approach is to call the company and get a directory that lists its officers, quarterly financial statements, and other public information.

The JobBank series published by Bob Adams is available in many bookstores. These books are guides to local employers in various areas. *The Denver JobBank* lists the names of primary employers in the Denver area. In the introduction, a brief overview of the economy in Denver is presented, including job trends. This is followed by listings of employers in various industries, including accounting and auditing, advertising, marketing and public relations, aerospace, amusement, arts and entertainment, and so forth. In addition to Denver, JobBank books are available for Atlanta, Boston, the Carolinas, Chicago, Dallas–Fort Worth, Detroit, Florida, Houston, Los Angeles, Minneapolis–St. Paul, New York, Ohio, Philadelphia, Phoenix, San Francisco Bay Area, Seattle, St. Louis, Tennessee, and Washington, D.C. They can be ordered from Bob Adams, Inc., Center Street, Holbrook, MA 02343.

What are you looking for in your information search in addition to who might hire you? A way to get your foot in the door, a selling point, an attention getter? Yes. Are there operations that can be "outsourced," an euphemistic term for subcontracting? Businesses are constantly looking for outsourcing opportunities because of the overhead associated with health insurance, retirement plans, and other similar costs. Are there more efficient ways to get things done? Is there an unrealized market? Is there a way to increase productivity? There is no greater attention-getter than to be totally informed and to tell the person that you are talking to that you believe you can make a valuable contribution to his or her business. The subtle message should be, "You need me to enhance your efforts, to save you money, to make you more successful, or to enhance the functioning of your organization."

Creating your own job through cold calls does not require high-pressure tactics. The name of the game in business is to make money, and if you can make a contribution to this process, you will be welcomed.

Concentrate on small businesses

One final piece of advice: start with small businesses, those that have fewer than 250 employees. The directories I listed above categorize companies by size and can be an invaluable resource. Jobs are not being created by Fortune

500 companies any longer. Additionally, and probably unfortunately for these companies, they are more wed to the tradition of hiring young workers and training them according to established procedures. Small businesses are more flexible and typically do not have the human resources available in large businesses. Go right to the top of smaller businesses, because that is where hiring occurs.

Newspaper Advertisements

Many job seekers report frustrating results when responding to newspaper listings of jobs. However, in this day of equal opportunity employment jobs, particularly those in the public sector, jobs must be advertised extensively, and newspapers are a favorite personnel recruitment device. The problem with newspaper advertisements is that they may be so brief as to give you few clues about what the employer is seeking. The following advertisement recently appeared in a southern newspaper:

> We are looking for a person with people, marketing, and management skills to develop a unique food store for the XYZ area. Send resume to POB 666, Atlanta, GA area.

This advertisement probably resulted in numerous responses, because many people see themselves as having people, management, and marketing skills. It is likely that the successful candidate will have experience in food retailing, however. Should you pursue this type of advertisement? Only if you are prepared to receive a lot of rejection letters. However, if you can demonstrate that you have all the skills except the experience in the food retailing area, you might give it a shot.

You will increase your chances of getting a job if you respond only to those newspaper advertisements that spell out in detail what qualifications they are seeking in candidates. Contrast the advertisement above to the one that follows:

> Apparel company seeks vice-president of finance and administration. Successful applicants should have a minimum of 10 years' experience in the apparel industry with knowledge of cost accounting, financial reporting, strategic planning, and employee benefit administration. Send resumes to VP for Finance and Administration, POB 1778, Burlington, VT.

This advertisement gives you an explicit set of criteria by which you can judge the likelihood that you will be a competitive candidate: 10 years of experience and certain definite skills. The question often becomes, "Should I apply if I do not meet all the criteria?" The answer is probably, particularly if you meet most of the criteria. Few job searches result in the location of the ideal candidate, and generally, some of the qualifications listed are more important than others. For example, it is unlikely that the employer would insist on 10 years of experience for the job listed above if a candidate were exceptionally strong in the other areas listed.

Which newspapers should you consult? Obviously that depends on the geographic locations you are targeting. However, high-level positions such as CEOs and vice-presidencies may be advertised nationally in newspapers such as the *New York Times,* the *Los Angeles Times,* and the *Chicago Tribune* or regionally in newspapers such as the *Washington Post* or the *Atlanta Constitution.* Advertisements for hard-to-fill jobs such as systems analysts, software developers, certain types of engineers, and other technical jobs will also be placed in wider, more geographically diverse newspapers. Sometimes employers will recruit from areas where there are concentrations of certain types of workers. An advertisement for aerospace workers might be placed in newspapers in Southern California, Houston, and Seattle because of the concentration of engineers and technicians associated with the aerospace industry in these areas. The Silicon Valley located in Northern California might be targeted for recruiting programmers, systems analysts, and computer technicians. The most extensive listings of jobs will be in the Sunday editions, and you may be able to acquire these at your local newsstand. However, if that is not possible, call the circulation department of the newspaper, and they will gladly help you subscribe to the paper.

Electronic Classified Ads

High technology has made its way into the job hunt, but in order to participate fully in accessing this approach you should have a personal computer, a modem that will link you to electronic data bases, a printer, and a fax machine. You must also be willing to spend a few more dollars than you would for your local newspaper. E-Span is an electronic on-line service that contains extensive listings of corporate, governmental, and health care jobs that may not be available from other resources. However, you cannot access the on-line service directly. You must subscribe to one of a number of electronic bases, including GENIE (800-840-4569), CompuServe (800-848-8990), and America OnLine (800-827-6364), among others. For a complete listing of data bases and their costs contact E-Span at 8440 Woodfield Crossing, Suite 170, Indianapolis, IN 46240.

E-Span offers an indirect way to subscribe to the service. For a fee of $14.95, they will provide you with a diskette that lists approximately 1,200 job openings from across the United States. In order to subscribe to this service, call the 800 number listed above. They require that you pay in advance, either by credit card or check. If you are interested in this resource, I suggest that you purchase one diskette initially to determine if it meets your needs. You will immediately see that E-Span job listings contain much more information than the classified ads in newspapers. This allows you to make a more accurate determination of your qualifications for the job and gives you an opportunity to prepare a resume, cover letter, and interview strategy to get the job. If the diskettes do meet your needs, then I suggest that you purchase one diskette every other week until you have achieved your objective of obtaining a job. For a listing of other electronic data bases, see appendix A.

Public Employment Services

The U.S. Department of Labor, in association with the state departments of labor, operates an extensive system of public employment agencies known variously as Job Service, Manpower Services, or Employment Security Offices. These agencies are funded by the states but have access to data from the entire United States, regardless of where they are located. Because of their affiliation with the U.S. Department of Labor, local employment offices can access regional and national job information. Employers list jobs with these agencies, and job placement officers try to locate suitable candidates for those jobs. In order to use this service, all you need to do is to call your local office for an appointment to register. The registration procedure requires that you provide information about your work history as well as your career goals. In some states, personnel in these offices provide career counseling as well as services such as resume development and job interview training. Employment security offices are unlikely to be helpful if you are looking for a supervisory or managerial position, because most businesses use other approaches to fill these jobs.

Private Job Placement Offices

Private job placement offices have been in existence for decades. However, the number of these offices has increased dramatically over the past decade, primarily because job seekers have been unable to negotiate the labor market on their own and public employment offices have not met the demand. Many private employment offices provide excellent services. However, the attorney general of the state of New Jersey received 10,000 complaints in one year about deceptive practices in these agencies. There have also been documented cases of widescale rip-offs in California and elsewhere. Generally, the fraudulent or misleading practices are centered in two areas: making unsubstantiated claims about success and requiring large registration fees with no commensurate follow-up to help the registrant acquire a job. Respectable agencies will provide you with a list of employers who have hired people from them and job hunters who have secured jobs as a result of registering with them. Make sure that you check the references of the agency before you pay a large registration fee. Belonging to national professional organizations may be an indication of the quality of services provided and the integrity of the staff, but it is no guarantee. If you have any questions about the reputation of the agency, check with the consumer services section of your state's attorney general office to see if complaints have been lodged against the agency. Typically, private employment agencies are licensed by the states in which they operate, and the attorney general's office will have records of complaints and actions taken regarding those complaints.

Private employment agencies, like their public counterparts, have jobs listed by employers who are seeking qualified workers. Unlike their public counterpart, their service is based upon a fee for service. In some instances, the employer pays the fee, and in other instances, the successful job hunter underwrites the cost. Usually the placement agency will make this information available to you at the time you contact them. If they do not, be sure to ask. Typically the agency's fee is the equivalent of one-twelfth of the first year's salary (one month's salary) and must be paid whether you work for the entire year or not. You will be asked to sign a contract at the time you register with the agency. Read it carefully before signing, because it will invariably spell out your financial obligation.

Head hunters

Some public employment agencies specialize in the procurement of certain types of employees, such as top-level managers, experienced engineers, and scientists. In some instances, these agencies are referred to as "head hunters," because they may aggressively recruit workers who are not necessarily looking for work at the time by contacting them directly. For the most part, head hunters work for the business, not the client. However it is possible to register with a head hunter in the hope that you will be the type of person one of their clients is seeking. Employers usually pay the head hunter's fee, except for a small registration fee. Again, before you register with a head hunter, make sure that you check the references of the people involved in the agency and never give them large sums of money up front. The National Job Campaigning Resource Center located in Panama City, Florida, will, for a fee, provide you with lists of the top head-hunting and job-placement firms in various industries. Acquiring these lists would be an ideal place to start if you wish to use a private job placement agency.

Temporary Placement Agencies

Temporary jobs are discussed in another section of the book. However, it is important to note that many temporary jobs turn into permanent ones. The serious job hunter will register with temporary placement agencies. Consult the yellow pages of your telephone book for a full listing of these agencies. You can also obtain a directory that lists the members of the National Association of Temporary Services by writing 119 South Saint Asaph Street, Alexandria, VA 22314. However, because the cost of this directory is expensive ($135), I recommend that you stick to your local telephone book.

Professional Organizations and Trade Associations

When you retired, you may have dropped your membership in professional and trade associations. Before you activate your job search, re-enroll in these associations. Check to see if the association you are joining offers lower membership rates for retired members—many do. However, you need membership in these organizations for two reasons.

First, they typically publish newsletters that contain job listings. You will want to receive these primarily because the jobs listed are most likely to be in your field. Second, you also need to be able to list these associations on your resume to demonstrate to employers that you are still on the cutting edge of your field.

College Placement Offices

Many colleges and universities offer job placement services for alumni, typically for a fee. Check with your alma mater about the types of services they offer. Determine if they have a service that will provide you with listings of job openings as they receive them from employers. Also ask if they provide resume development advice and job interview training. Since it is unlikely that you are still in the same geographic area as your alma mater, you will also want to determine if they have reciprocal arrangements with other colleges that would allow you to use services closer to home. A few private colleges have established these types of relationships.

Obviously, college career placement offices are not going to be a primary source of information about job openings for retired job hunters. However, if you feel the need to improve your letter-writing, resume, and job-interviewing skills, these agencies may just be the source of help you need.

Job Fairs

The unemployment rate in the Triangle area of North Carolina where I live stands at 2.5 percent currently. Recent newspaper articles have addressed the shortage of skilled workers in a variety of areas. Recently, as one means of recruiting new workers, several area businesses conducted a job fair in Raleigh, North Carolina. At the job fair, which was organized by the North Carolina Employment Security Division, dozens of businesses set up booths staffed by people who were there to explain the nature of their business and to discuss opportunities for new employees. This job fair was advertised throughout the state of North Carolina in newspapers and on the radio. It was also advertised in newspapers in Atlanta, Washington, D.C., and in the *National Business Employment Weekly* calendar of events. Hundreds of workers attended the fair in search of new or first-time jobs.

A job fair represents an unusual job-hunting opportunity and should not be missed. It is a job hunter's market;

the employer is recruiting you. Attend with business cards and resumes ready. Visit every booth that looks promising. Leave a business card. Collect the information that is made available about businesses. Get the names of recruiters and as many other names as possible. Determine the best means of follow up. Should you call or write?

After the job fair:

- Organize your notes and prioritize the order that you will contact businesses. What businesses seemed to offer the most promise? Who are the contact people?

- Redo your resume to fit jobs. Emphasize skills employers are seeking.

- Write letters expressing your interest in jobs that were discussed, or make telephone calls if that is more appropriate. If you write, enclose another resume.

- If you made contacts with businesses that do not have openings that fit your credentials, write letters thanking them for the opportunity to discuss their company. Enclose your resume and tell them that you would be interested in working with them if jobs develop in the future.

- Establish dates for follow-up.

Electronic Resume Pools

One of the relatively new approaches to the job search involves listing your resume in an electronic data base. E-Span Job Search Database currently charges $19.95 to list a resume on their service. They recommend that the resume include key words that reflect language usage, machines that you can operate, and other skills. Employers can access the data base to identify prospective professional, managerial, and technical employees.

One feature of the E-Span Database is that you can select either an open or confidential approach. If you have an open listing, your resume will be sent to any employer requesting it. If you have a confidential listing, you will be given the name of the requesting employer; if you agree, only then will your resume be forwarded to the employer.

Summary The first step toward securing a retirement job is locating vacancies that match your credentials. This task will require an extensive effort on your part, an effort that will involve using networking and consulting newspaper advertisements as well as those listed in professional and trade publications. It may also require the use of private and public employment agencies, registering with a temporary employment agency, and attending job fairs. The most difficult but potentially rewarding approach to locating retirement job openings is through cold calls that focus on developing the job you want. The use of this approach requires you to do extensive research about the businesses that you will be approaching so that you can convince them that you can help enhance the success of their business.

The Retiree's Resume

7

Did you know that most employers spend about one minute with each resume they receive?

Your resume is a one-minute introduction to you and your job skills. Because employers spend so little time with the resumes they receive, how you prepare your resume is crucial. However, before I address the actual development of your resume, I want to review three basic approaches to resume development. One is obviously to prepare one yourself with the help of this chapter and perhaps two or three of the dozens of resume development guides on the market today. Another method is to use one of the software packages available on the market to supplement your efforts. These packages, which sell for $10 to $89 are ingenious resources, but they require that you be somewhat familiar with the use of a personal computer. The third approach is to hire a professional consultant, usually a career counselor, to help you with this chore.

If you choose either the first or second option, you certainly will need the information presented in this chapter. If you choose to use a consultant to help you develop your resume, make sure that you choose a reputable person. I recommend that you first look for a person who is a nationally certified career counselor (NCCC). These professionals have at least a master's degree in counseling that includes courses and supervised work in career development. They have also completed the course work needed to provide personal counseling and passed the examination required to become a nationally certified counselor as well. In order to continue as NCCCs, they must engage in continuing education in the career counseling area. To get a list of NCCCs, call the National Board of Certified Counselors in Alexandria, Virginia.

The Basics Of The Resume
Making it age proof

In their book *The Over-40 Job Guide*, Kathryn and Ross Petras discuss the so-called age-proof resume. This idea looks good in the table of contents of a book, particularly to workers who are worried that they will not be hired because of their age. There is discrimination out there, but don't allow yourself to think that you can fool employers about your age by developing one type of resume instead of another. However, the Petra's are right in one regard: you shouldn't call attention to your age in your resume. However, neither should the 22-year-old. The purpose of the resume is to illustrate that you have the skills and the personal attributes needed to perform the job.

It is also important to remember that, as an older worker, you have several advantages over the younger worker. Maturity, experience, and stability are your selling points, and your resume should stress these points. You can do this best with a functional resume. More about this type of resume later.

Filling the gap

If you are retired and did not enter a retirement career immediately, you have a gap in your resume. A gap is a time when you were unemployed, and you can get lots of advice about what to do about the problem that may result because you spent some time out of the work force. My advice? Don't get terribly concerned about gaps in your resume. Concentrate on your positive attributes. However, in your cover letter and in the interview, you will need to explain why you have been out of work and what brings you back to the job market at this time. Do not try to fill gaps with superfluous activities.

Overqualified?

"Being overqualified" for a job is a phrase that has always mystified me. How can a person be too qualified to perform any task? Actually you can't. But some employers worry that if you take a job that is too easy by virtue of your experience and training, you will be bored and either not do the job well or leave it altogether after a short period of time. In the next section I will recommend that you use a functional resume instead of a chronological one. One reason is that a functional resume allows you to present the information that is relevant to the job you are seeking, thus leaving out information that might lead an employer to conclude that you are overqualified. In the final analysis, you should be the one to decide if you are, in fact, interested in a position.

Resume styles

There are three types of resumes:

- Chronological—information such as educational and employment histories are listed by dates in reverse order, that is, listing the most recent events first.

- Functional—information is listed in terms of functions performed and skills developed or utilized.

- Mixed—aspects of the functional and chronological resume styles are combined.

Although the chronological resume is the most popular style, probably because it is the easiest to develop, employers prefer the functional. All three styles of resumes will be discussed, but the functional resume is recommended for the retiree for several reasons, not the least of which is that it is preferred by employers. Moreover, the functional resume gives experienced workers the opportunity to show off their skills and experience and can easily be customized to correspond to the job being sought. The chronological resume makes it very easy for an employer to do a quick estimate of the job seeker's age (the dates listed for her or his first job will give her or him away) before she or he can show her or his stuff. One of the things that we know about prejudiced people is that they typically hold group stereotypes, and these images often break down on a one-to-one basis. At this point, all you want to do is have an opportunity to challenge those irrational beliefs about older workers. Finally, the functional resume allows the applicant to avoid being tagged as overqualified and thus eliminated from the candidate pool.

Some authors recommend that people who are re-entering the workplace, such as housewives and retired workers, use functional resumes to hide the "holes" in their work history. This type of recommendation simply indicates that many "experts" underestimate the abilities of employers. Research has shown that employers are not fooled by functional resumes. Therefore, be forewarned, if you have a hole in your work history, you are going to have to explain it sooner or later because employers are going to pick it up. My suggestion is that you address the reason you dropped out of employment in the cover letter.

Truth in packaging

Honesty is the preparation of your resume is not the best policy—It is the only policy. Because many companies have been burned by dishonest job seekers, employers typically check all information presented on a resume before hiring a person. If you do falsify employment history and it comes to light after you are hired, you will be fired, regardless of the contribution you are making. The resume should be a statement of the facts and only the facts.

One to two pages in length

In discussing the resume for the over-40 crowd, Kathryn and Ross Petras recommend that you not concern yourself with the length of your resume. I couldn't disagree more. There are many things that are debatable in the job search area, but resume length is not one of them. The resume should be one to two pages in length. Why? Because the typical employer spends only a minute or so on each resume. Your task is to present a one-page billboard that is boiled down to an 8½-by-11-inch piece of paper. To do this, you must eliminate the superfluous, minimize the marginal, and highlight the essentials. Highlighting is typically done by underlining or with the use of bullets.

Expensive paper, clean format

There has also been a great deal of discussion about the type and color of the paper the resume is printed on. The rule is that it should be tasteful, which means white, buff, gray, eggshell, or a similar color. The paper should also be a heavy bond, 20 pounds or more. Also, there is no disagreement about whether the resume should be typed or hand written. Unless you are applying for a job as a finger painter, type your resume. Better yet, use a computer and laser printer.

Job recruiters prefer resumes that have clearly defined career objectives, place headings on the left side, use action verbs to describe work experience, and look uncluttered. Additionally, employers deplore spelling errors, smudges, and messy documents. Brevity and neatness count. In his book *Resumes for the over 50 Job Hunter*, Samuel Ray recommends that you begin your resume with what he terms a career summary and place your specific career goal in your cover letter. This is an acceptable alternative if you include a cover letter with every resume you distribute. However, that is unlikely.

Resumes, not resume

You don't need a resume, you need resumes. In chapter 6, I mentioned the importance of establishing multiple job targets. Let us say that you are applying for jobs as an engineer, a sales representative of products requiring engineering expertise, and a management position in an engineering firm. The core knowledge and skill base of these jobs may be engineering, but each job also requires some unique skills that would need to be emphasized in separate resumes. With the aid of a computer software package or a good consultant, you can develop these resumes simultaneously.

Don't get disqualified because of sexist, demeaning language

Many people, particularly men, in the over-50 group were taught to use male pronouns to represent both males and females. That form is outdated and considered offensive by many people. Resumes should be either gender-fair or gender-free. The safest approach is to use plurals, such as *they* or *we*, rather than *he or she* or not to use gender at all. Contrast the following statements:

- Supervised 10 salesmen (sexist)

- Supervised 10 sales persons (acceptable)

- Supervised a sales staff of 10 people (acceptable)

Either the second or third statement would be considered correct, but the third one seems less cumbersome. Words like *workers, staff,* and *personnel* are gender-free. These gender-free words should be used even if everyone you are referring to is a male or a female. Of course, if you coached the Green Bay Packers, it would be all right to refer to them as the men on the team since it is widely understood that only men are allowed on the Packers. However, because there are few exceptions, the best approach is stick to non-sexist or gender-free terms. In this way you are always safe.

Never use the word *boys* or *girls* to indicate the gender of workers. Workers may be men or women, but they cannot be boys or girls in the modern workplace. To call adults *girls* and *boys* is demeaning and most employers will not tolerate it.

Finally, the use of nonsexist language becomes a real problem for some people, particularly with words and phrases like *man hours* and *man power.* A retired airlines pilot refused to use the phrase *person hours* or simply *hours* when referring to the time it took mechanics to repair airplanes. His contention: all mechanics are men. One day the plane he was on had a mechanical problem and could not take off. The mechanic who boarded was female. A friend asked, "I wonder how many man hours it will take for her to repair this plane?"

Exclude personal information   Never include your birthday, marital status and other family information, your Social Security number, race, religion, hobbies and other leisure pursuits, and height and weight in your resume.

Use bullets   The purpose of the resume is to call immediate attention to your strengths. You should do this by the use of bullets. For example:

- walks on water

- leaps tall buildings with a single bound

- worshipped by all employees

These are illustrations. Remember the principle about honesty.

Preparing To Write Your Resume
Work experience

Regardless of the type of resume you intend to prepare, begin by making a list of the jobs you have held in reverse chronological order, that is, the last job you held first, the next-to-last job second, and so forth. As you make this list, leave several lines between job listings so that other essential information can be inserted.

- Responsibilities of your job. Give details: what, where, and how many. What were your responsibilities, where were they carried out (if significant), and how many people, machines, states, countries, units were involved?

  Example: Manager of technical assistance throughout the United States for XYZ Computer Company.
  - Supervised the work
  - Coordinated the training of 30 technicians who provided telephone and field support for customers of XYZ Computers.

- Accomplishments on the job. What did you do to enhance the functioning of the people, production, or other processes for which you had responsibilities?

  Example:
  - Decreased customer complaints about technical support by 75 percent.
  - Increased sales production by at least 10 percent each quarter.
  - Decreased employee attrition by 35 percent as a result of an innovative employee relations program.
  - Reduced the number of rejects in the production process by 85 percent by installing electronic sensing devices.
  - Decreased late payments by 35 percent by installing automated calling service.

Complete the following worksheet and begin the process of preparing your resume.

Worksheet For Resume Preparation

Job 1. Title and company _____

Dates held _____

Major responsibilities _____

_____

Major accomplishments _____

_____

Reason for leaving job _____

_____

Job 2. Title and company _____

Dates held _____

Major responsibilities _____

_____

Major accomplishments _____

_____

Reason for leaving job _____

_____

Job 3. Title and company _____

Dates held _____

Major responsibilities _____

_____

Major accomplishments _____

_____

Reason for leaving job _____

_____

This worksheet contains spaces for only three jobs, but your worksheet should include spaces for all the jobs you have held throughout your life. A highly respected professor still lists brick mason's assistant on his resume, which illustrates in one sense why he has risen to the top of his field. He was not afraid to engage in hard work 35 years ago and still isn't. In the final resume, you may eliminate some of the jobs you have held or some of the tasks you have performed because they reveal little about you as a person or as a worker. But for now, do not discard anything.

Educational background

Now make a similar worksheet for your educational background. Starting with your most recent, list all educational experiences. Some people make the mistake of overlooking the various schools and training they have received during their career, falsely assuming that only educational experiences such as high school and college count. Those in the military know that at each critical step in their career there are preparatory schools that may stress leadership and supervision, logistics, interpersonal skills, self-understanding, and a host of other skills. People who have pursued civilian careers have often had similar training to prepare them as they moved from technical field to technical field, from labor to management, and from human resources to sales. The lessons learned in some of these schools may be more important to success in a new career than any college course. After each training experience, list whether a degree, certificate, or diploma was earned. If you completed high school, you earned a diploma. If you completed college or community college, you earned a degree. You probably earned certificates of accomplishment for your other educational experiences, although for brief training experiences, no diploma or certificate may have been awarded.

Licenses and certifications

Make a list of the licenses and certifications you hold and when they expire. These will need to be included on your resume if the jobs you are seeking require them. If they have lapsed, get them renewed or make plans for renewal.

Awards, professional and trade associations, and other accomplishments

Make separate lists of awards you have received; the associations to which you belong; and any accomplishments, such as inventions, patents, publications, prestigious consultantships, or invited presentations to prestigious organizations.

Career objectives

Make a list of your career objectives. Remember, the best way to be successful in the job hunt is to pursue multiple options. These statements need two components: the general title of the job you are seeking and an assertion about the contribution you can make to that job.

Recommendations

Identify at least three people who will provide positive written or oral recommendations that will support your career objectives. You may have a different set of recommendations for each job you intend to pursue. Contact each person before you place them on your list to make sure they are comfortable providing a positive recommendation. These names will not appear on your resume, but they may accompany the resume when it is sent to potential employers. Your resume will read, "Recommendations available on request." If a prospective employer requests references, be prepared to hand them out, fax them, or mail them.

Writing The Resume: The Problem

Now that you have identified all the crucial information needed to prepare a resume, you have a problem: putting together one page of information that will demonstrate that you are the type of person who can function in the job for which you are applying. With words, headings, bullets, and just the right amount of white space, you are going to paint a picture of a person who has been successful in the past and who will be successful in the future. Successful people are action-oriented, competent people who have high personal expectations, who produce at high levels because of those expectations, and who enrich both themselves and the people for whom and with whom they work.

Writing The Resume: The Solution

The resume has five sections: identifying information, career objective, educational experience, and work experience and references. Because you are not going to list your references but simply insert the line "available upon request," you will be concentrating on three of these sections.

Identifying data

This part is simple. List your name, address, and telephone number.

The career objective

List your specific career objective and a little about yourself here. If you include a career summary, as some recommend, you may get discarded because the employer is looking for a young sales person to train. Also, what if the employer is looking for a person with a diverse background in sales, and you have mentioned only your retail sales experience because that is your strong suit? You get disqualified. The purpose of the career objective is to have the employer read the rest of your resume so that you can present your entire case. Some examples of career objectives follow.

- Seeking a challenging position in retail sales.

- Programmer seeks position as programmer analyst where extensive knowledge of computer languages can be applied.

- Customer service position sought by individual with outstanding ability to deal with people.

- Experienced manager seeks part-time position in hotel industry.

- Seeking administrative assistant position where organizational and clerical skills can be utilized.

What is the common thread in these career objectives? They tell the employer what job is sought and something about the person's ability to do the job. Words and phrases such as *challenging, extensive knowledge, outstanding ability*, and *experienced* are there to pique the employer's interest. They invite the employer to read on, but they do not provide enough information to get you disqualified. If the employer does read on, you have a chance.

What is even more important about the career objectives listed above is that they identify specific careers. Employers hire people to meet specific needs, unless they are hiring trainees just out of college. Let's face it, you are not in this category.

Identify your skills

In the preceding section, you were asked to identify the jobs you have held, your accomplishments in those jobs, and to list your educational experiences. Now it is time to analyze these experiences and identify the skills you have developed as a result of your work and training.

Action verbs   You want to describe yourself as an action-oriented person. The best way to do this is to use action verbs in your resume. Action verbs are typically in the past tense because they describe things that you have done. You have led, organized, sold, designed. What follows is a list of action verbs that you can use in your resume. Think about the jobs you have held, the responsibilities those jobs entailed, and the accomplishments you listed above. Then go through the lists provided and identify action verbs that might describe how you interacted with people, how you dealt with data, what you did with things such as machines and animals, and what you did in relationship to ideas. Place a check beside those action verbs that might be useful to you in writing your resume.

Actions verbs relating to people:

_____ 1. acted	_____21. entertained
_____ 2. addressed	_____22. facilitated
_____ 3. administered	_____23. guided
_____ 4. advocated for	_____24. hosted
_____ 5. assigned	_____25. informed
_____ 6. cared for	_____26. innovated
_____ 7. coached	_____27. instructed
_____ 8. collaborated	_____28. interviewed
_____ 9. communicated	_____29. led
_____10. consulted	_____30. managed
_____11. coordinated	_____31. mediated
_____12. counseled	_____32. motivated
_____13. critiqued	_____33. organized
_____14. debated	_____34. planned
_____15. delegated	_____35. persuaded
_____16. diagnosed	_____36. recruited
_____17. directed	_____37. scheduled
_____18. disciplined	_____38. sold
_____19. educated	_____39. solicited
_____20. encouraged	_____40. taught

Other actions verbs that describe you in relationship to people: _____

_____

_____

Action verbs relating to data:

_____ 1. accounted		_____21. graphed
_____ 2. analyzed		_____22. inspected
_____ 3. appraised		_____23. interpreted
_____ 4. audited		_____24. organized
_____ 5. balanced		_____25. prepared
_____ 6. billed		_____26. presented
_____ 7. budgeted		_____27. reconciled
_____ 8. calculated		_____28. recorded
_____ 9. collected		_____29. reported
_____10. compared		_____30. researched
_____11. compiled		_____31. scanned
_____12. coordinated		_____32. summarized
_____13. copied		_____33. systematized
_____14. developed		_____34. transmitted
_____15. dispensed		_____35. typed
_____16. displayed		_____36. updated
_____17. estimated		_____37. utilized
_____18. explained		_____38. validated
_____19. filed		
_____20. forecasted		

Other actions verbs that describe you in relationship to data: _____

_____

_____

Action verbs involving things such as machines and animals:

_____ 1. activated	_____20. handled
_____ 2. adjusted	_____21. inspected
_____ 3. appraised	_____22. laid out
_____ 4. assembled	_____23. maintained
_____ 5. built	_____24. mapped
_____ 6. catered	_____25. modified
_____ 7. collected	_____26. monitored
_____ 8. constructed	_____27. navigated
_____ 9. controlled	_____28. operated
_____10. decorated	_____29. painted
_____11. designed	_____30. processed
_____12. demonstrated	_____31. produced
_____13. displayed	_____32. programmed
_____14. drafted/drew	_____33. regulated
_____15. enlarged	_____34. repaired
_____16. exhibited	_____35. restored
_____17. experimented	_____36. synchronized
_____18. fed	_____37. timed
_____19. fixed	

Other actions verbs that describe you in relationship to things: _____

_____

_____

Action verbs involving ideas:

_____ 1. conceived	_____11. innovated
_____ 2. created	_____12. invented
_____ 3. decided	_____13. investigated
_____ 4. defined	_____14. perceived
_____ 5. developed	_____15. prioritized
_____ 6. devised	_____16. resolved
_____ 7. discovered	_____17. solved
_____ 8. forecast	_____18. understood
_____ 9. formulated	_____19. validated
_____10. imagined	_____20. visualized

Other action verbs that describe you in relationship to ideas: _____

_____

_____

Using action verbs

In the previous section you were asked to identify the jobs that you held, the responsibilities associated with those jobs, and your accomplishments on those jobs. You should describe your responsibilities and accomplishments on your resume using action verbs and paint a picture of your skills. For example, if you are a software engineer looking for employment, you might describe your programming knowledge and skills like this:

- Skilled in the utilization of C++ to solve development programming problems. Three years of programming experience using COBOL and ORACLE.

This description tells prospective employers that you have the skills to use three currently popular computer languages to develop software programs.

Former bookkeepers might describe their skills as follows:

- Utilized Lotus 1-2-3 and AccPac Plus to keep corporate books, including accounts receivable and accounts payable.
- Organized and managed bookkeeping systems for corporations ranging in size from 20 to 340 employees.

The key to describing yourself is to use action-oriented verbs that tell what you can do in a succinct fashion. Remember, you are shooting for a one-page billboard.

Putting It All Together: Sample Resumes

Three sample resumes for the same retiree are presented here. These resumes represent the chronological, the functional, and the mixed types of resumes.

FIGURE 7.1

The Chronological Resume

Larry G. Nash
613 Applecourt Lane
Greensboro, NC 27516
919-555-6767

POSITION

Residential Real Estate Sales Position Offering Opportunity for High Sales Volume

PROFESSIONAL
EXPERIENCE
1973 to 1992

Better Homes and Gardens Realtors, Inc.
Memphis, Tennessee
Salesman
Sold residential real estate concentrating primarily on middle- and upper-income housing. Led company in sales volume nine of nineteen years. Led company in residential real estate listed ten years during the same period. Designed open-house program and other marketing strategies.

1953 to 1973

United States Army, Quartermaster Corps
Entered as enlisted man; retired as captain. Commanded 120 men. Primary responsibilities were in supplies procurement and warehousing.

1950 to 1953

Various part-time jobs during high school—newspaper delivery, checker in supermarket.

EDUCATION

George Washington High School, Fort Worth, Texas—Diploma, 6/1/55

University of Maryland, College Park, Maryland—B.A. in business, 6/12/61.

North Memphis Community College, Memphis, associate's degree in real estate sales, 12/15/93

PROFESSIONAL
SKILLS

AWARDS
• Distinguished service medal, 1967
• Kiwanian of the year, 1981
• Memphis real estate salesman of the year, 1982

REFERENCES

Available upon request.

FIGURE 7.2

The Functional Resume

Larry G. Nash
613 Applecourt Lane
Greensboro, NC 27516
919-555-6767

POSITION

Residential Real Estate Sales Position Offering Opportunity for High Sales Volume

PROFESSIONAL SKILLS

SKILLS
- Designing real estate sales campaigns, including newspaper advertisements and direct mail sales. Created innovative open-house program that increased sales by 12 percent.
- Residential real estate appraisal. Developed checklist of 20 easiest ways to increase the value of your home.
- Developing creative real estate financing approaches. In last position identified 28 million dollars in untapped financial resources for home buyers.

AWARDS
- Memphis real estate sales person of the year
- Company leader in sales volume nine years; company leader in listings 10 years
- Memphis Kiwanian of the year award for service to the community

PROFESSIONAL EXPERIENCE

Better Homes and Gardens Realtors, Inc.
Memphis, Tennessee
- Residential sales
United States Army, Quartermaster Corps
- Entered as enlisted man; retired as captain

EDUCATION

George Washington High School, Fort Worth, Texas
Diploma

University of Maryland, College Park, Maryland
B.A. in business

North Memphis Community College, Memphis, Tennessee
associate's degree in real estate sales

REFERENCES

Available upon request.

FIGURE 7.3

The Mixed Resume

Larry G. Nash
613 Applecourt Lane
Greensboro, NC 27516
919-555-6767

POSITION

Residential Real Estate Sales Position Offering Opportunity for High Sales Volume

PROFESSIONAL EXPERIENCE

1973 to 1992

Better Homes and Gardens Realtors, Inc.
Memphis, Tennessee
Residential real estate sales person

1953 to 1973

United States Army, Quartermaster Corps
Entered as enlisted man; retired as captain.

1950 to 1953

Various part-time jobs during high school—newspaper delivery, checker in supermarket.

EDUCATION

George Washington High School, Fort Worth, Texas
Diploma

University of Maryland, College Park, Maryland
B.A. in business

North Memphis Community College, Memphis, Tennessee
associate's degree in real estate sales

PROFESSIONAL SKILLS

SKILLS
• Designing real estate sales campaigns including newspaper advertisements and direct mail sales. Created innovative open-house program that increased sales by 12 percent.
• Residential real estate appraisal. Developed checklist of 20 easiest ways to increase the value of your home.
• Developing creative real estate financing approaches. In last position identified 28 million dollars in untapped financial resources for home buyers.

AWARDS
• Memphis real estate sales person of the year, 1982
• Company leader in sales volume nine years
Company leader in listings 10 years
• Memphis Kiwanian of the year award for service to the community

REFERENCES

Available upon request.

The resumes listed in figures 7.1, 7.2, and 7.3 illustrate the three types of resumes. The chronological resume listed in figure 7.1 uses plenty of white space, gives the person's work and educational history, uses a combination of underlining and bullets to highlight certain aspects of the resume, and identifies some of the key skills needed in real estate sales. However, it contains sexist language (e.g., salesman), definitely inappropriate. It also contains some useless information, the high school work record, which also tips off the reader to the age of the job applicant. Perhaps even more importantly, it fails to highlight the skills of the applicant.

Figure 7.2 contains a functional resume that immediately calls attention to the applicant's skills and accomplishments using bullets and underlines. It leaves out the useless information regarding high school employment. It doesn't include dates, although it makes reference to extensive experience in real estate sales and a fairly long stint in the army. Any experienced employer can guess that he or she is dealing with an older worker, but age is not the central focus on the resume: skills and accomplishments are.

The mixed format resume presented in Figure 7.3 presents all of the essential information and does a better job of highlighting the accomplishments of the applicant. It could be improved by reversing the "skills/accomplishments" sections and the "work history" sections and by eliminating the high school employment information. Also notice the "professional skills" and "awards" sections. The accomplishments and awards sections have an irregular pattern of indentation that deviates from the rest of the resume without adding anything of significance. The result is a resume that looks a bit sloppy.

A Final Note

Earlier I mentioned computer programs that will help you in preparing your resume. Two to consider are:

Easy Working Resume Creator (about $20)
    Spinnaker Software Corporation
    201 Broadway
    Cambridge, MA 02139

Resume Maker (about $50)
    available from Career Research and Testing
    2005 Hamilton Avenue
    San Jose, CA 95125

As you would expect, Resume Maker provides many more options for preparing your resume than does Resume Creator. In addition to providing more flexibility, it assists you in writing job-search letters, keeping track of your job-search activities, and gives you tips for job hunting and interviewing. However, if you just want to do a quick resume, Resume Creator may be all you need. Check out software stores for these and other resume programs.

Summary   The resume is an essential job-hunting tool that deserves a great deal of attention. Whether you decide to seek the help of a professional or do it yourself, certain principles should be followed. Resumes should be relatively brief (1 to 2 pages), neat, typeset or laser printed, and conservative (paper should be white, buff, or gray and at least 20-pound bond). Importantly, they should call attention to your skills and accomplishments, not how long you have worked. You want to demonstrate that you have had 25 years of experience and accomplishments, not one year of experience 25 times. Finally, you should develop resumes, not a single resume. Computers provide you with the opportunity to customize your resume to highlight your skills. As an experienced worker, you have probably developed the skills to perform many jobs. You need one resume for each of those jobs.

Job Search Letters for the Retiree

Did you know that a recent study sponsored by AARP supports the long-held belief that employers discriminate against older workers?

The focus of chapter 7 was developing a resume. However, unless a resume is handed directly to an employer, it must be accompanied by a cover letter. Just as you need more than one resume if you are a serious job hunter, you need several job search letters. For example, if you decide to engage in an all-out letter-writing campaign to contact employers about job openings they have now or in the future, you will need a "hire-me-now-or-in-the-future" letter, sometimes referred to as a broadcast letter. If you are following up a lead provided by an individual in your job hunt network, you will need a networking or "they-told-me-to-contact-you" letter. When you answer an advertisement about a job vacancy, a cover letter for your resume or a "please-interview-me" letter is appropriate. You will also need some standard follow-up or "Why-haven't-I-heard-from-you?" and a "thank-you-very-much" letter. An informal-style thank-you letter was described in the networking section of chapter 6, but a formal thank-you note will be discussed and illustrated here.

Some General Considerations Style

You probably remember the regimen of writing business letters from your high school English class. They should be dated, have an inside address, a return address, a salutation followed by a colon, a body, and a closing. They should be typed (word processing and a laser printer are better) on high-quality bond paper (20 pounds or better), single spaced, have generous margins, and be free from grammatical and spelling errors. Furthermore, the paper should be 8½-by-11 inches. Please, don't use an odd-sized stationery that can get lost on the desk of a busy employer.

Making your point

Business letters should also be businesslike, that is, straight to the point—the facts, the whole facts, and nothing but the facts. You need to make your point and shut up.

But what is the best way to make your point? One way to make your point is to use high-quality printed stationery that is the same color and paper weight as your resume. Even if you are applying for a job that requires you to get greasy up to your neck every day, your cover letter–resume package should look neat. This communicates to the employer, "I cared enough about the job to take the time to try to impress you." Additionally, printed stationery eliminates the need for a return address, because your address is on the letterhead.

Be positive

You can also make your point by being upbeat, positive. I'm a great person. You have a great company. If we can get together, the result will be increased greatness for both of us. It may sound a little sickening, but it isn't. It is using what my grandfather called "soft soap" and what advertising executives call the "soft sell." And make no mistake about it, you are selling something. You are selling yourself, and you are your own advertising executive.

Language

Avoid sexist language. This point cannot be stressed enough. Make your letter gender-free, and it will demonstrate that "You've come a long way toward enlightenment," to paraphrase the Virginia Slims advertisement.

The Points to Cover
Tell what you want

The opening paragraph of your cover letter should state your career objective and then provide a brief statement of why you are the best person to do the job. Employers hate to read letters just to find out why you are writing. If you are writing about a specific job, then identify the job title. if you are writing a "hire-me-now-or-in-the-future" letter, the objective may be more general. Two examples follow.

Specific Objective
I am seeking a challenging position as a mortgage loan processor. I have extensive experience in mortgage loan processing and packaging. I function best in fast-paced work environments that allow me to make the most of my well-developed organizational skills.

General Objective
I am seeking a senior management position in a rapidly growing business in the finance industry that will allow me to draw on my extensive managerial experience and problem-solving ability.

Brag—Tell them why you can do the job

The opener should be followed by a summary of your qualifications and a quick overview of your major accomplishments. Listing your major accomplishments is actually a marketing section and is essential. In this paragraph it is also a good idea to mention that you are re-entering the labor force after retirement, if that is the case. This fact should not be in the opening paragraph. Dazzle the employer with your potential, then ease into the fact that you have been retired. When disclosing that you are a retiree, try to turn what may be a negative into a positive. Either in a subtle or not-so-subtle fashion, let the employer know that the no-work retirement life-style is not for you.

The ugly topic of money

Believe it or not, there is more consternation among job hunters about salary expectations than any other topic. If you have a minimum salary expectation, be sure to include this in your letter. However, talk of money should be postponed until the end of your letter. The reason? The employer may have a salary figure or, more likely, a salary range established for the type of job you want. If your minimum salary exceeds the established range, your letter and the attached resume may be discarded before you are ever seriously considered. If you are not overly concerned about salary, the old flexible line "My expectations are that the salary will be commensurate with the responsibilities of the job," will suffice. All you are saying with this line is that you expect to be paid the same as other people doing the same job and that money may not be the primary factor in accepting the job.

Ask for an interview

Always ask for an interview. Nobody gets hired on the strength of her or his cover letter or resume. The purpose of the resume and job-hunting letters is to produce a positive bias, one that will lead employers to want to take a closer look.

Thanks for your consideration

Close every letter with a "thank-you-for-considering-me" sentence. This is common courtesy.

Hire-Me-Now-or-in-the-Future Letter

In spite of the odds, which are generally considered to be 200 to 1 against getting a job this way, some job hunters insist on a letter-writing blitz that covers every employer that might conceivably offer them a job. An AARP-sponsored study published in the *Bulletin* in February of 1994 found that 90 percent of people writing these types of letters received out-and-out rejection letters in return. The researchers also found that older workers were somewhat more likely to receive rejection notices than younger workers. The letter blitz is an expensive and frustrating job-search method, but (and this is what keeps job seekers doing it) some people get jobs this way. If you do decide to use this approach, you need a well-designed letter and a resume. The letter must demonstrate to prospective employers that they are not the recipient of a letter from a desperate job seeker who is contacting 450 of the Fortune 500 companies and giving them an exclusive opportunity to hire the world's greatest worker. The only way to do this is to do extensive research about the company and target the company's needs, not your own. Remember, employers hire people to make them money.

Your research should identify the following information:

- Company name and location

- CEO's name

- Products produced / services provided

- Target market / market share

- Types of workers employed

- New initiatives, if any

- Names of people who can hire you

Resources that you can use to get information about employers were listed in chapter 6 and will not be repeated here. However, you should consider the electronic data bases listed in appendix A as sources as well as financial analyses such as those provided in Standard and Poor's, which is available in many libraries. Ultimately you will need to make some discreet telephone calls to the company or agency to get the name and address of the person or persons whom you should contact. "To Whom It May Concern" cover letters do not get jobs.

Another example of a hire-me-now-or-in-the-future letter is presented in Figure 8.2. In this letter, the retiree has undergone retraining.

FIGURE 8.1

Hire-Me-Now-or-in-the-Future Letter

John G. Harding
411 Sunset Drive
Albuquerque, NM 87102
505-555-8155

March 28, 1994

Ms. Camila Adler
Regional Sales Manager
Funtime SportsWear, Inc.
811 West Champion Street
Albuquerque, NM 87101-811

Dear Ms. Adler:

I am seeking a position as a sales representative in your company. I have over 25 years of successful sales experience, largely in the area of wholesale sales. I also operated a retail sporting goods outlet for five years, so I understand the perspective of the retailer. This gives me an important advantage in this competitive market.

I am contacting you because in researching companies that might offer the opportunity I seek, I discovered that you are about to launch a new product line aimed at the "over-40 crowd." This is an unusually shrewd move because of the disposable income of this group and the data that suggest they are increasingly engaged in leisure activities. I would like to have the opportunity to work as a sales representative in what will undoubtedly be a successful venture.

I have been an outstanding sales person throughout my career. I retired last year and moved to New Mexico, but I find that I miss sales. I intend to continue my career as quickly as I can find a suitable position. As you will see in the enclosed resume, I have extensive sales experience in the clothing business, the last 15 years of which were with the Nike clothing division. You will also see that I won several awards for my sales activities. However, the accomplishment that I am proudest of is that I was over my sales quota every year during my tenure with Nike.

My compensation requirement is in the $40,000 range. However, because I am confident that I can sell your product, I am not opposed to working on a salary-plus-commission basis as long as my potential earnings are in the high forties.

I am most appreciative of your consideration of my credentials, and I am looking forward to meeting you to discuss career opportunities.

Sincerely,

John G. Harding

FIGURE 8.2

Hire-Me-Now-or-in-the-Future Letter

Joseph Clark
6913 Willow Park Street
Maypole, Ohio 42466
207-555-901

November 3, 1993

Mr. Jonathan Kile
Alliance Auto Repair
1616 Cedar Avenue
Colleyville, OH 43588

Dear Mr. Kile:

I am seeking a job as a tune-up mechanic in a repair shop that utilizes the latest in diagnostic equipment, and I have learned that your shop is one of the most up-to-date in the area.

I have worked in the field of auto repair for many years. Eighteen months ago I retired from Goodguys Chevrolet, where I worked as a tune-up mechanic. I soon learned that retirement was not for me, so I enrolled in the advanced auto mechanics class at the community college, where I am happy to report that I finished at the top of my class. Now I am ready to return to work in a state-of-the-art tune-up shop.

A resume that lists my experience and skills is enclosed. I am a highly reliable employee who really enjoys working on automobiles. Please call me so that we can discuss how I can make a contribution to your operation.

Thank you for considering my application.

Sincerely,

Joseph Clark

FIGURE 8.3

They-Told-Me-To-Contact-You Letter

Patricia J. Harris
13 Old Patriot Way
Boston, MA 02494
617-555-6868

July 26, 1993

Ms. Anne Finkelstein, Senior Editor
Simon Little Publishing Group
12 Lookout Place
Suite 16
Boston, MA 02400-012

Dear Ms. Finkelstein:

I recently had the opportunity to discuss my desire to secure a job in book editing with Gerrard Harold, who is employed in your division. He suggested that I contact you about positions within Simon Little. Specifically, I am seeking a position editing science fiction, although I am interested in editing other areas of fiction as well.

Until recently I served as editor of the science fiction collection for Pegasus Publishing Company. During my tenure in that job, I expanded their science fiction list and made it a highly profitable line, and I am confident that I can make a similar contribution to your company. My strengths lie in discovering new authors and seeing that manuscripts are developed in a timely fashion.

I have enclosed a complete resume for your perusal. You will note that I retired from Pegasus Publishing approximately one year ago. Since that time, I have found that I miss the excitement associated with the publishing business and the satisfaction associated with contributing to the growth of a company. My research indicates Simon Little is a small company that has gradually expanded its fiction line and that it may be ready to accelerate its growth. If my assumptions are correct, I can make a substantial contribution to this area because of my contacts with authors and my ability to find new talent.

My salary requirements are flexible, although I would expect to be paid a salary that is commensurate with the responsibilities of the job.

Please call me if you currently have or anticipate an opening on your editorial staff. I am looking forward to the opportunity to discuss how I can make a contribution to your business.

Thank you for your consideration.

Sincerely,

Patricia J. Harris

They-Told-Me-to-Contact-You Letter In many instances your networking efforts will yield this type of recommendation: "I'm not sure whether they have anything, but contact Jerry Lanning—and tell him I told you to write." These letters contain the same information as the please hire-me-now-or-in-the-future letters, with one exception: There has to be some mention of the referral source, because that legitimizes your letter. It really is that old foot-in-the-door technique, and that is why this type of letter is somewhat more effective than the letter arising from no lead at all.

Follow-Up Letters If you decide to send a letter to everyone who might have a job opening, you may elect to select a group of employers for a strategic follow-up. You may also wish to follow up some of your "they-told-me-to-contact-you" letters. Normally these letters are brief, reassert your interest in employment, restate your career objective, and end with an invitation to call and a thank-you. Wait at least two weeks before sending these notes. You don't want to become a pest. One example of this type of letter is shown in Figure 8.4.

FIGURE 8.4

Follow-Up Letter

Mr. Robert Engle, Executive Vice-President
Charter Industries
1109 Parkhurst Avenue
Farmington Hills, MI 49632

February 20, 1994

Dear Robert:

Three weeks ago I wrote to you soliciting your help in my job search at the suggestion of Tom Wise. As you probably recall, I have decided to return to work after a year's hiatus and am seeking a position as corporate planning analyst. I've enclosed another resume that details my qualifications.

I'm excited about returning to a corporation such as yours. I realize that you may not have an opening, but if you do not, I'd appreciate any leads that you can provide.

Thank you in advance for any help you may provide. I appreciate your consideration, and I hope to hear from you soon.

Sincerely,

Jane Q. Job Hunter

Thank-You-Very-Much Notes

When you receive assistance from anyone, immediately send a thank-you note. This note, in addition to expressing appreciation, should encourage them to keep you in mind and to send you other leads. Figure 8.5 is one example.

FIGURE 8.5

Thank-You Note

September 9, 1993

Mr. Robert Engel, Executive Vice-President
Charter Industries
1109 Parkhurst Avenue
Farmington Hills, MI 49632

Dear Robert:

I was disappointed to learn that you are not anticipating any openings that might be suitable for me, but I do appreciate the suggestion that I call Larry Thompson at GHQ Accounting. I followed up immediately, and Larry was quite receptive. We have an appointment to discuss the needs that GHQ has and how I might meet those needs.

Although I have an appointment with Larry Thompson, I will continue to actively seek a job until I find suitable employment. If any other employment possibilities come to mind, please contact me.

Thanks again for your help.

Sincerely,

Jane Q. Job Hunter

Please-Interview-Me Letter

These letters are usually referred to as cover letters because they are sent as "covers" for your resume. They are written in response to advertisements for help wanted in newspapers, trade and professional publications, and electronic data bases.

Analyze the advertisement

Before you begin your letter, carefully analyze the job advertisement. How many years of experience are they asking for? In what types of positions? In what industries?

What specific skills are requested? After you have conducted your analysis, look at your resume to determine if you have highlighted those aspects of your experience and skills so that they correspond to the hiring requirements of the advertised job. If you have not, redo your resume. Also make a list of accomplishments that you wish to mention in the cover letter.

Dealing with deficiencies

One of the tricky tasks that you must handle when you are applying for a job for which you are not fully qualified is how best to address deficiencies. Conventional wisdom has been to dance around the issue and hope the employer is so dazzled by your other qualifications that he or she will not notice your deficiencies. In his book *175 High-Impact Cover Letters,* Richard H. Beatty writes that cover letters may take two forms: linear or literary. The linear approach, according to Beatty, is the traditional approach when the worker has the qualifications needed to do the job that has been advertised. It is written in the form "I can do the job because . . ." followed by several lines that list your qualifications. The literary approach is taken when the author does not have all the qualifications yet wishes to draw attention to his or her own parallel experiences. Beatty suggests that employers are much less likely to be aware of deficiencies if the literary approach is used. This is nonsense. Attached to the cover letter is a resume that outlines your qualifications. You can only cover up so much with a cover letter.

If you are applying for a job for which you are not fully qualified, I suggest that in the paragraph that contains your qualifications you begin by listing all qualifications that correspond to those listed in the advertisement. Then you should suggest that you do have some deficiencies and that these may not make a difference in your job performance or that they can easily be remedied.

For example, many advertisements specify that the candidate have a minimum amount of experience, perhaps 10 years. Typically this number is established arbitrarily in an attempt to make certain that candidates have the minimum experience needed to function effectively in the job. A deficiency in this area might be addressed as follows in a response to an advertisement for a quality assurance engineer. The following paragraph would follow a list of your qualifications for the job.

> I noted the advertisement specified that a minimum of ten years in quality assurance and employee relations work experience is a prerequisite for candidates. I am confident that the eight years of experience I have will allow me to perform at an exemplary level because of the depth and diversity of that experience. The details of this experience are listed in my resume. However, I want to direct your attention to the special schooling that I have completed in this area and my extended visits to several Japanese companies to study their quality assurance procedures.

But what if you do not have one of the skills listed in the advertisement? Remember that when job descriptions are created, employers hope to fill as many voids as possible. Because of this, they may create a job description for a unicorn—something that doesn't exist. If you have most of the skills listed in the advertisement, be sure to stress that you are highly skilled in these areas and that you are a quick study, that is, you can acquire the skills needed. If no unicorn applies for the position, you may get the job by virtue of being a close approximation of a unicorn. You are the best qualified worker in the applicant pool.

Also, when reading job descriptions, be aware of two key words: *preferred* and *essential.* If employers indicate that they prefer certain word processing skills (e.g., Microsoft Works), they are leaving the door open to people who may not be proficient in this area. If the advertisement indicates that a skill is essential and you do not have it, you have only two choices: don't apply or find a way to get the skill immediately. If you are applying for a job where you are deficient in an essential skill, such as the use of a software package, you might insert the following paragraph into your letter after a list of your qualifications.

> My qualifications are identical to those listed in your advertisement, with the exception that I am not fully acquainted with dBase software at this time. However, I am enrolled in a course at the JQP Community College that addresses dBase software and thus will be proficient in this area shortly.

Why call attention to your deficiencies? Because sooner or later, the employer will find them. If you call attention to them, you have the opportunity to rebut or preempt the negative reaction that may result when the deficiencies are discovered. You can use the literary approach and pray that your deficiencies will not be discovered. You can use the direct approach and give yourself a fighting chance to make your case.

Overqualified?

One of the classic problems confronting the retired worker is that they are just too darned qualified. As I have stated, it is hard for me to consider the idea that someone is too qualified, but, realistically, some employers tend to discount applicants who are applying for jobs for which they appear to have too much experience or training. If you feel that you might be perceived as overqualified, you should not call attention to this in your cover letter. It should simply state how your qualifications match those listed in the advertisement. For example, if the job announcement indicates that candidates should have more than five years of experience and you have 20 years of experience, simply indicate that you have more than five years of experience. If it suggests that you should have a certain skill level and you exceed that level, just indicate that you meet the skill level listed. For example, if an advertisement asks that candidates have the ability to deal with a certain type of software and you have many other skills in this area, point out that you have the skills identified in the advertisement and are proficient in the use of a number of software packages.

The purpose of the cover letter is to get employers to read your resume. Let them see how really capable you are when they discover all of your skills and talents.

Finally, with regard to overqualification, it would be possible for you to go back and "dumb down" your resume to make you look less qualified than you are. I recommend against it, primarily because we do not know whether being overqualified is actually a detriment in the hiring process. Until we get past the conjecture stage on this issue, let's assume that more is better.

Figure 8.6 is an example of a cover letter. Although this sample letter is written to a specific person, it may well be that your cover letter will be written to the business. Why? Because many newspaper advertisements do not contain names. A recent advertisement for an internal staff auditor simply advised prospective employees to write to Folio GM Heavy Truck Corporation and gave an address.

FIGURE 8.6

Please-Interview-Me Letter—
Applicant Has Qualifications

Lorraine E. Swift
16758 Broadway
Indianapolis, IN 57766

Mr. Clarence Brown, Supervisor
Clark and Associate
300 Circle Way
Indianapolis, IN 57665

Dear Mr. Clark:

I am interested in the position of administrative assistant advertised in the *Indianapolis Star* on December 21, 1994. I have enclosed a resume for your examination.

I am highly skilled in data entry, have extensive experience with WordPerfect for Windows, and am highly proficient with Lotus 1-2-3, which are the skills you list in your advertisement. I am also proficient with several other types of software packages, which are listed in my resume. Just as importantly, I am a cheerful, highly reliable worker who is equally effective working as a team member or alone.

My salary requirements are in the $15,000 range.

Thank you for considering my application. I would welcome the opportunity to discuss how I can make a contribution to your company with you.

Sincerely,

Lorraine E. Swift

FIGURE 8.7

Please-Interview-Me Letter—
Applicant Does not Have All Qualifications Listed

Larry D. Brownell
66 Roosevelt Lane
St. Louis, MO 56680

PDQ Chemical Corporation
Post Office Box 777
St. Louis, MO 56678

Dear Madam/Sir:

I am submitting my resume in response to your advertisement in the *St. Louis Dispatch* on March 4, 1994, for a director of sales and marketing. The job sounds ideal for a person with my experience and training.

My specific qualifications for the job include:

- B.A. and M.A. in marketing

- Over 20 years of marketing and sales experience

- 10 years of management experience, including 5 years at the senior level

- proven record of ability to motivate people; increased sales in my last position over 20 percent per year

I also note that your position announcement indicates that sales experience in the chemical industry is highly preferred. My experience has been primarily in the automobile industry, specifically in the marketing of tires. Prior to writing this letter, I conducted research into your company and found that some of your customers are in the automobile and related industries. My knowledge of marketing strategies for this group would give me an edge in this area, and I am confident that I could quickly gain the knowledge needed to develop successful sales strategies for your other customers. As my resume will confirm, I have a record of continuous success in marketing, ranging from salesperson of the year three times and regional sales manager of the year four times.

I would anticipate receiving a salary in the neighborhood of $75,000.

I am excited about the possibility of discussing your opening with you directly. Thank you for considering my application.

Sincerely,

Larry D. Brownell

What if you do not have many of the skills asked for in the advertisement?

Don't apply unless you have too much time and money on your hands; employers hire people to solve problems. If they hire an unqualified person, they have simply created more problems. I am not saying that unqualified people have never gotten jobs. I am saying that it is an extremely low-probability job-search strategy. Stick to the high-probability approaches already discussed.

Summary

In order to conduct an effective job search, you will need a wide array of letters. Remember, these letters are surrogates; they represent you. If they are poorly done, it says something about you, the job hunter. Spelling and grammatical errors characterize you as a sloppy person. Sexist language indicates a lack of sensitivity. Not writing thank-you notes may indicate indifference. These are not the impressions you wish to make.

I have recommended that you depart from tradition in one important way: when you have a deficiency, address it head on. However, there are some traditions that should be followed. State your career objective and tell why you are qualified. Give a list of your major accomplishments. State your salary requirements, always ask for an interview, and thank the employer for her or his consideration of you.

The Job-Winning Interview: Never Let Them See You Sweat

Did you know that in the job interview, negative information receives twice as much weight as positive information in the final evaluation process?

Over 50 and Interviewing

It may have been a long time since you last interviewed for a job, and if you are like most Americans, you have never been trained how to succeed in the job-interviewing process. If you have looked around, you know that there is no shortage of resources that tell you how to succeed in this process. Because you may not have interviewed for a job in recent years, this chapter will begin with a general discussion of the interview process. This discussion will be followed by a look at how this

151

process applies to the retired worker, which in turn will be followed by some specific suggestions about how you can succeed when you interview for a job.

Overview of the Interview Process

I have read dozens of popular books on the interview process. Generally, they urge you to knock 'em dead (Yate), put dynamite in your answers (Krannich and Krannich), or adopt some other strategy that will allow you to overpower the interviewer. The authors of these books then proceed to give you a "few" pointers to carry with you into the interview process. Krannich and Krannich offer 45 surefire principles that will allow you to blow interviewers out of the water, stand on their chests, and bellow like Tarzan because you have defeated them and they have offered you a job. Yates offers suggestions on how to flash your eyebrows, move your mouth, hold your head, cross your legs, sit, fold your arms, maintain eye contact, and mirror your interviewer's nonverbal behavior on your way to defeating the interviewer. That is just in one chapter. Both these books and others describe the interview in adversarial terms.

I take a different tack in this chapter, although I agree with many things that are said in these books. I will reduce the interview process to its lowest possible denominator by making the fewest number of recommendations possible. You can entertain only three to five pieces of information at one time and fewer than that when you are stressed. There are some things that you should think about before the interview so you won't have to think about them during the interview such as grooming, dress, and organization of your materials.

I will also argue that a collaborative attitude is the best tack to take when interviewing. I am adamantly opposed to the adversarial approach advocated in many self-help books which go so far as to recommend that you try to fake psychological tests. Why? Because the workplace has changed. Employers want people who will fit into a work team. The interview is the place to begin demonstrating that you can do just that.

Goals of the Interview
The interviewer: avoid hiring mistakes

The job interviewer has two basic goals: to determine whether you can do the job and do it in a fashion that is acceptable to the company. Every company has an image that it wishes to project and a culture it wishes to protect.

When Apple and IBM negotiated some collaborative efforts, both image and culture clashed. Apple has developed an informal culture were employees are encouraged to dress casually and interact in the same way. Its image is one of innovation and creativity. IBM, or Big Blue as it is often called, operates very formally and is more bureaucratic. The image it tries to project is competence and leadership. A computer scientist who interviews with these two companies will have to recognize these differences and accommodate them in the process.

Because interviewers often have many candidates for the same job, they are looking for reasons to disqualify you, and thus the interview is a search for negative information. Each candidate is rated on a series of factors such as interpersonal skills, ability to do the job, emotional maturity, ambition, and appearance. These ratings are then summarized into a more global rating that may be like a grading system (A, B, C) or, more simply, a recommendation for probable action (not interested, have a follow-up interview, make an offer). Figure 9.1 is an interview rating form that is based on the forms used by a number of interviewers.

Interviewee's goals: impression management

The technical term for the interviewee's goals is *impression management,* and we know that the key to this is careful interview preparation. First and foremost on the interviewee's list is to communicate that he or she can do the job. Most companies will overlook a few idiosyncrasies if they believe a worker can perform at a high level. Additionally, interviewees must demonstrate that they have the interpersonal skills needed to work collaboratively. The new workplace requires that employees work together to achieve goals. While this is the much ballyhooed Japanese management style, the fact is that the collaborative approach was developed in this country. The Japanese have developed it to a fine art, however. Regardless of the origin of the idea, most employers want employees that can function independently and can work in teams.

Do you know why most people are dismissed from their jobs? It isn't for lack of competency. It is because they cannot get along with other people in the work setting. This, of course, relates to the ability of employees to work collaboratively, but it also relates to their ability to respond appropriately to supervision, settle personal disputes amicably, and generally be a positive force in the workplace. So you must prove that you can do the job, that you will fit

FIGURE 9.1

Candidate Rating

Candidate's Name _____

Position for which candidate is being considered _____

Date/Place of Interview _____

Factors (rate on a 1 to 5 scale with 1 being poor or weak and 5 being strong or exceptional)

APPEARANCE

dress   grooming   manners   neatness   appropriateness

INTERPERSONAL SKILLS

handshake   eye contact   posture   assertiveness   poise

warmth   openness   humor   sensitivity

COMMUNICATION SKILLS

listening skills   fluency   thoughtfulness   grammar

animation   succinctness   persuasiveness

MOTIVATION

ambition   commitment   goal oriented   energy level

INTERVIEW PREPARATION

knowledge of company   knowledge about job

INTERVIEW BEHAVIOR

confidence   response to questions   questions posed

organization   punctuality   genuineness

LEADERSHIP

ability to influence others   charisma   work ethic

attractiveness   decisiveness   task orientation

maturity   objectivity   problem/solving ability

intelligence   willingness to assume responsibility

ATTITUDE TOWARD WORK

enthusiasm   independence   dedication   loyalty

commitment   punctuality   reliability   discipline

realism   competitiveness   upward mobility   ethics

team orientation

SKILL MATCH

formal preparation   experience   trainability

_____

Comments: _____

_____

_____

_____

Overall Rating: do not offer _____   possibility _____   offer _____ into the culture of the organization, and that you have the interpersonal skills and emotional stability needed to maintain harmony in the work setting.

Some Special Concerns

While it is often subtle and prohibited by law, many businesses practice discrimination against older workers. The bias that gives rise to this discrimination grows out of the stereotype that older workers are rigid, have lower energy levels than younger workers, do not learn as fast as their younger counterparts, and may be more susceptible to health problems. With the exception of the health issue, these ideas are unsupportable. Even in the area of health, older workers are less likely to have debilitating mental health problems than younger workers. This is probably because of their achievement of some stability in their lives and because of their maturity. Regardless, it is the responsibility of older workers to prove that they can be an asset and should be hired in place of younger workers.

Retirees have another burden in the interview process: explaining why they are either coming out of retirement or leaving one job and starting a second career. In this case, the stereotype of retirees may actually work in their favor. A common belief is that retirees soon wither and die because they miss their jobs so much. While this is bunk, many interviewers will be sympathetic to the person who chooses not to retire. An interviewing principle for the retiree is to challenge negative stereotypes and leave positive ones intact.

Types of Interviews

From the interviewee's perspective, interviews are generally of two types: group and individual. Both group and individual interviews may be conducted by a single interviewer or by a panel of interviewers. The objective of the interview is to hire competent employees, but in order to accomplish this goal, prospective employees may be subjected to a series of interviews. The first of these, the screening interview, may be conducted by telephone in a few instances but is usually conducted face-to-face by a personnel officer. The candidate rating sheet shown in figure 9.1 might be used to summarize the results of this interview. The screening interview is typically the only interview used to hire blue collar workers. It is also used by small businesses, by colleges and universities to hire professional staff, and by governmental agencies. In these situations, the screening and hiring interview are the same. However, public schools, hospitals, and many businesses follow up the screening interview, which is conducted by a personnel office, with a hiring or placement interview that is conducted by the person in charge of the school (principal), the department (chair), or unit (manager).

The primary purpose of the hiring interview is to determine the compatibility of the prospect with the work group. In highly technical work settings, the interviewer is also trying to determine whether the interviewee possesses the technical knowledge and skill needed to succeed. It is likely that the prospective worker will be subjected to a series of interviews that may be conducted by an individual or groups in hiring interviews. The bottom line is that the person who hopes to succeed in the job interview process must be prepared to cope with a number of interview situations. The good news is that with a few exceptions, the rules are always the same.

The telephone interview

Some companies conduct telephone interviews. The purpose of this interview is to establish that you have the basic credentials needed to function in the job. What is difficult about these interviews is that you do not have the full range of nonverbal behavior to cue your response. The positive aspect of telephone interviews is that, except for some preliminary greetings, you do not have to worry about making a good impression. If you are going to be interviewed by telephone, make sure that you:

- Do a thorough investigation of the job and company prior to the interview.

- Understand each question that is posed prior to answering it. Ask the interviewer to repeat the question if you find it necessary to reflect, then respond. Never answer a question that you do not fully understand.

- Answer requests for negative information carefully.

The group interview

In almost every instance where there are multiple interviewees, there are multiple interviewers. In a few instances you may not know who the interviewers are at the outset of the interview, but this is unusual. Some businesses use the group interview both to save money and as a means of determining how a candidate functions in a social setting. For example, American Airlines uses a group interview to screen prospective flight attendants because there are at least 10 qualified applicants for each position, and a flight attendant must be able to function at a high level in dynamic social situations. Typically 80 people walk into these interviews, and 8 are selected.

A few simple rules will suffice if you are subjected to a group interview:

- As soon as you enter the group setting, start introducing yourself and meeting people. Don't be a wall-flower and let people come to you.

- Be cheerful. Smile.

- When sitting in a group, sit across from the interviewer. Your chances of getting hired are increased (if you function well).

- Listen to everyone. When you answer a question, talk to everyone. Don't just focus on the interviewers.

- Follow the other suggestions in this section.

The Interview Process Preparation

The old saying "Success is one-tenth inspiration and nine-tenths perspiration," can be paraphrased to read "Success in interviewing is one-tenth inspiration and nine-tenths preparation." If you do not prepare properly for the interview, you cannot perform well or, to put it differently, if you are going to ignore this section of the chapter, ignore the other sections as well. The question is always where to begin. While this order is arbitrary, I suggest that you (1) investigate the employer, (2) explore the job that you are seeking, (3) develop a plan to sell yourself that will include how to dress, and (4) develop some preliminary answers to questions.

Investigating the employer

Interviewers expect you to know something about their business or agency when you present yourself for an interview. The question is, "What should you know?" The following list was compiled to answer this question and assist you in exploring a business.

Company Name _____

Name of CEO _____

Location of corporate headquarters _____

Location of major subsidiaries _____

_____

_____

Major products/services produced _____

_____

New products planned _____

Market niche _____

Market share _____

Number of plants/sales outlets _____

Market potential _____

Profitability _____

Profit forecasts _____

Debt and asset allocations _____

Stock price and recent fluctuations _____

Competitors and their products _____

_____

Getting this information can be relatively easy. Begin by asking the person who has contacted you to send the latest quarterly and annual report to stockholders. Then, if you have a stockbroker, call and ask him or her to consult Standard and Poor's or Moody's for additional financial information about the company, including its credit rating. By reading the *Wall Street Journal,* you can get stock price trends. *Forbes* and *Fortune* magazines publish annual evaluations of all major corporations, and these can provide useful information about the company. Publications such as *Value Line* can also provide useful information about the company, its products, its past, and its future. Some public libraries subscribe to this publication. Every stockbroker will have access to it. Even if a company is privately held, it will produce annual statements about its financial well-being, which will be made available to you if you ask.

If you are exploring a governmental agency, public school, college, or university, the information that you are seeking is somewhat different. The following guidelines should be useful in your search for information.

Name of agency _____

Name of head of agency _____

Location of agency _____

Location of other offices/campuses _____

Size/enrollment _____

Trend in size or enrollment _____

Population served _____

Trends/changes in population served _____

Primary mission of agency _____

Funding of agency (last three years) _____

Projections for future funding _____

The information needed for the exploration of a governmental agency or other public institution is typically available only from the agency. This means that you should ask for this information by calling the public information officer of the agency or by sending a request to the person who contacted you about the job.

Exploring the job/work setting

Just as you are expected to have a great deal of information about the business or agency for which you hope to work, you are also expected to know a great deal about the job for which you are interviewing. The following outline can help you in your exploration.

Job applied for _____

Name of interviewer _____

Telephone number of interviewer _____

Address of interviewer _____

Job title of interviewer _____

Duties of workers in this job _____

_____

Initial training required _____

_____

Type (formal or on-the-job) _____

Compensation range _____

Fringe benefits _____

_____

Typically, prospective employers have already provided you with a job description if you have been asked to interview. However, if that is not the case, get a description. If there is a published salary scale, get that as well along with comparative information, if it is available. Also ask for the name of another employee in the same position who would be willing to discuss his or her job with you. An accountant with one of the Big Six accounting firms has found that the difference between the expectations and reality of new hires in her field are tremendous. Engineers, management and sales trainees, lawyers, teachers, and nurses make similar reports. New flight attendants and commuter airline pilots may qualify for food stamps, something they did not expect. Unless you talk to another employee (perhaps more than one), you may miss important nuances about the job that will determine your satisfaction. Moreover, any information that you learn about salary and fringe benefits can help you negotiate a salary if you are offered a job later.

Dressing for the interview The goal of dressing properly is to have the interviewer realize that you are right for the job the moment he or she lays eyes on you. One rule of thumb here is dress as though you were going to work, only a bit better. Don't wear a suit if you are interviewing to become a mechanic. Conversely, don't have grease under your fingernails if you expect to become an executive. A second rule is dress so carefully that you do not have to be concerned about it in the interview. You will have many other things to worry about during the interview, so put this one aside prior to the event. Rules regarding dress for interviews vary a bit for men and women. However, the best way to determine how to dress is to talk to someone on the inside. Men can be well dressed on any college campus in the United States in a blue blazer, a white or blue button-down shirt, a striped or paisley tie, a gray pair of pants, and a pair of wing-tipped shoes. For women, the "uniform" is a blue blazer, a plain white blouse with or without a conservative scarf, a gray skirt, flesh-colored hose, and black flat or low-heeled shoes. Of course variations are accepted, but the emphasis is on dark and conservative. Most insiders can give you a quick overview of what is acceptable and what is not.

I once sat in on a board meeting of a medium-sized pharmaceutical company. I was wearing a dark suit, as was every other male and female in the room except the chief corporate attorney. On that day he elected to wear an attractive but bright gray sport coat; a white shirt; black trousers; black loafers; and a black, red, gray, and white tie. His outfit was tasteful and expensive. However, there were at least 15 remarks in a span of two hours that made note of how sharp he looked or were pointedly derisive. My point? Make sure there are no negative comments about your dress on the interviewer's rating sheet. This is an area where you can easily get all high marks.

Typically, men should wear dark, single-breasted suits (solid, pinstripe, or muted plaids) that are made from wool or wool blends. Silk and linen blends should be avoided as should polyester, but for different reasons. Some silk and all linens wrinkle easily, and it is impossible to make a good impression if you look as though your suit and pajamas are one and the same. Polyester shines and generally looks cheap. When you are dressing to impress, cheap is out. Shirts should be cotton or cotton blend and may be white, blue or gray and may have light stripes as long as they blend nicely with the suit and tie. The tie should be the standard popular width, silk, and conservative.

You have undoubtedly heard much about power ties, ties that project an image of personal authority. Typically power ties are red, although some more conservative groups, such as engineers, prefer burgundy power ties. While I personally witnessed an overnight conversion to red ties after an organizational consultant mentioned that red projected authority, the fact is that in the realm of body language, the color of the tie has a miniscule impact on how people perceive you It is far more important that the tie be tastefully selected, tied carefully in a small knot, and blended with the suit and shirt.

The shoes should be black or brown to match the suit and newly polished. Shoes, like the remainder of the outfit, do not have to be new. However, they should be free from scuffs and should at least have new heels. Scuffed shoes, frayed clothing, and spots on clothing or ties are forbidden. Hosiery should be black or brown, depending on the color of the shoes, and should be mid-calf length.

The rules for women are very much the same as men. Suits should be dark; blouses should be plain (free from ruffles); scarfs, if worn, should be conservative and should blend with the outfit. Shoes should be flat or have a low heel. As is the case with men, clothing should reflect contemporary standards, and that includes the length of the skirt. This is not to suggest that miniskirts are acceptable, even if they are in vogue. Knee-length and longer is the rule for skirts. Both men and women should take into consideration their body build and other characteristics before choosing clothing. If men are portly, they should make sure that the suit fits nicely. Women who have problems such as varicose veins should probably opt for longer skirts. Regardless of your preference, women should wear panty hose. Because panty hose must have been invented by a man who didn't like women, they tend to develop runs and other flaws at absolutely the worst times. My advice is to stick an extra pair in the inside pocket of your attache case, which, incidently, is preferred to a purse in interview situations.

Jewelry for women, like their clothing, should be conservative. No dangling or large earrings. Small pearl or gold earrings are safe. No costume jewelry such as large watches or bracelets. Small gold or silver bracelets, small watches, and small rings are acceptable. Men who wear jewelry should also lean to the conservative side. Leave your diamond-studded earring at home.

Grooming for the interview

Hair. Beards, moustaches, and long hair for men are the topics of much conversation in some books, but as long as beards and moustaches are neatly trimmed and hair is clean and combed, they pose no problems. You will want to avoid looking like an aging hippie. There is nothing quite as pathetic as a person who does not age gracefully, and since many interviewers may be younger than you are, you are sure to get low marks in this area if your hair and beard are not age-appropriate. If you are balding, don't try to make three hairs cover your bald head. A shiny dome is preferable to a feeble attempt to disguise the fact that you are almost totally bald. Hairstylists recommend that as you bald you cut your hair shorter, particularly around the bald area. Many men grow moustaches and beards as they bald, and some even shave their heads. If you are considering these alternatives, do them long before you go to an interview so you won't be worrying whether you look good. You will have too many other things to worry about to be concerned about your looks.

Women should have conservative hairstyles that correspond appropriately to their facial features. Generally, short hairstyles are most acceptable, but if you have long hair and wish to keep it, French twists and buns are acceptable ways of putting up your hair. Prior to the interview, you may wish to try two or three hairstyles and get some feedback from friends and others about which looks best. *Best* in this situation means most conservative and most flattering.

Should you dye your hair? If you have been doing it, continue to do so. Don't go in with your roots showing. But what if you haven't been coloring your hair? Should you start? Men more than women are confronting this question, and the answer is "It depends." If dying your hair will help you make a better impression, go for it. If it will make you feel better about yourself, just do it. However, if coloring your hair is going to make you self-conscious, forget it. Gray or salt-and-pepper hair can be an asset in some situations.

Fingernails. Fingernails should be clean and neatly trimmed for men and manicured for women. Both men and women may wish to see a nail specialist just prior to the interview. Women who wear false fingernails should make sure that they take a repair kit with them on the day of the interview.

Fragrances. Women may wear fragrances. Men may not. The line "They will remember your fragrance long after you are gone" applies here. Unfortunately, if you are a male, the memories are not positive ones. Women should make sure that the perfumes they wear have a subtle scent. The interview is not the time for your perfume to elicit visions of Liz Taylor or Charlie. You want them to remember you.

Makeup. Makeup is acceptable for women but not for men. Prior to going to an interview, consult a makeup specialist to make certain the types of makeup you use match your skin tone. Also, acquire a conservative shade of lipstick and apply it lightly.

Your body   *Weight.* Take off all your clothes and stand in front of a mirror. Take a look from the front, the side, and the back. Now dress as you might for an interview and do the same thing. Will your clothes cover the body flaws that have developed over the years? People feel better about themselves when they are in good shape physically. This may be the time to join the health club, go on the diet you have been planning, start walking a mile or two per day, or change to a low-fat diet. Remember, your goal in the interview is to make a good impression. Even being a few pounds overweight can be a problem, but being 15 or more pounds overweight conjures up the image of a person on the way to a heart attack or, at the very least, a person with low energy. Remember the stereotype you are trying to dispel. One of the easiest ways to do this is to be lean and mean or thin and svelte. A cautionary note is in order here. If you are large-boned and have been a large person all your life, don't try to change nature. I'm only talking about losing weight if you have put on a few, or more than a few, extra pounds over the years. If you are on a low-fat diet or in an exercise program, it will help you preempt one of the interviewer's concerns.

Plastic surgery. This may seem to some to be going off the deep end a bit, but the miracles of modern surgery can help us look better. Hair transplants, liposuction, tummy tucks, face lifts, and the like are readily available for a price. Should you submit to plastic surgery to get a job? It depends on how badly you want a job. You will be competing against younger people for many jobs, and you just might have a tuck here and there if you think it will improve your confidence and your appearance. It is probably easier and certainly less expensive and better for you to go on a diet and start an exercise program.

A physical examination. I recommend that you get a complete physical examination prior to going to an interview and that you take the result with you to the interview. This allows you to answer any questions that may come up about your health with confidence and allows you to preempt any concerns the interviewer may have in this area.

The Interview

Preparation is complete. You know the company, and you can tell the interviewer in detail what the job is and how you can do it. It is time to consider the interview process itself.

Pre-interview

Make sure that you place a few extra resumes and a copy of the results of your physical examination in an attache case. Also, pack documents that will support your claims of past achievements and job performance. If you have received letters of commendation or your awards have been written up in the newspaper, copy these and take them with you. If you were "restructured" out of a job, also carry a letter of reference from your last supervisor. Place all of this material in alphabetized, clearly marked folders. Remember, you are going to be "graded" on your organizational ability. More importantly, in the middle of a stressful situation, fumbling around looking for material that you know you have will only add to your stress.

Arrive a few minutes early. If you can help it, never be late for an interview. If the unforeseen happens (e.g., an accident or your car stalls) call immediately to say you will be late. As you are sitting in the waiting area, pay particular attention to your heart rate and breathing. If you control your breathing, you will not have sweaty palms, a sure sign of anxiety. To control your breathing, simply concentrate on your diaphragm (the muscle under your rib cage) and fill your lungs completely from the bottom, then exhale very slowly. You will feel calmer, your hands will not perspire, and your head will be clearer, because when your anxiety level goes up, your ability to recall and process information is reduced.

The first five minutes

As you step into the interview, leave thoughts about clothing, grooming, and preparation behind. Make sure your panty hose doesn't have runs or your fly is zipped and get ready to go for it. You have done the best you can to get ready. Now is the time to concentrate on the interviewer and the job at hand: presenting yourself in the best possible light.

Research strongly suggests that many interviewers make up their minds about the viability of a candidate in the first few minutes of an interview. This is why appearance is so important. So greet the interviewer (male or female) with a firm handshake and a smile. Also be positive from the outset. Thank the interviewer for the opportunity to interview, tell him or her that you are very interested in the job and that you are excited about working for the company. Affirm that you can do the job and do it well. All of this should occur before the interviewer asks any questions. After two minutes, you have demonstrated that you are punctual, organized, positive, and enthusiastic.

You also want to establish an open, collaborative pose in the early part of the interview. Begin with a statement such as, "I know you are interested in finding out as much about me and my ability to help your company as possible. I'm here to give you that information because I honestly believe that I can do the job and do it well."

During the early moments is also a good time to present documents that support your accomplishments and the status of your health. A statement such as the following will suffice:

Interviewee: I brought some documents that I thought might help you evaluate my potential for the job. I listed some of my achievements on the resume, and this folder contains some additional information about those achievements. I also brought the results of a recent physical examination. Before I interviewed, I wanted to take every step to ascertain that I can perform at a high level, so I had a physical. I know that most companies are concerned about their health costs these days, so I wanted you to know that I am in excellent health. I also brought extra copies of my resume if you need them. (The message you have communicated is, "I'm interested, organized, and in good health.)"

Nonverbal behavior. There are four things to remember here. Smile, make eye contact (in our society, we think people are being dishonest when they don't, even when they are just shy), and sit comfortably with a slight forward lean (this makes you seem more open and approachable). Finally, don't fidget with your hands or feet (this is a sure sign of anxiety).

The middle portions of the interview

Typical interview questions. Now it is time to give the interviewer a shot at asking some questions. In some instances, interviewers will ask direct, closed questions, such as "What were your specific duties in your last job?" or "Have you ever had responsibility for monitoring a budget?" At other times they may ask more open-ended leads, such as "Tell me about yourself." Another type of open-ended lead or question may be posed such as presenting a problem for you to solve. An example of this is, "Recently, one of our departments had a tremendous amount of interpersonal conflict, and eventually, the personnel divided into two groups that were virtually at war. How would you have solved that problem?" In answering any of these questions, answer as fully as the question dictates, but do not volunteer additional information. For example, you want to tell exactly how you would resolve the personnel problem, but you do not want to criticize the department head for allowing the situation to get that bad in the first place. You could volunteer that after you solved the problem you would put certain types of mechanisms in place to make sure that the situation would not occur again in the future.

Stress interviews. Interviewers may also use several so-called stress interviewing techniques. If you are in a situation where the warm, inviting interviewer suddenly seems cold, hostile, or detached, you may be in the middle of a stress interview. Nonverbal cues, such as lack of eye contact, are also indicators that a stress interview is in progress. This approach is used because most interviewers know that candidates for jobs prepare for interviews. The stress interview is one means of breaking through a facade that was developed in this preparation. One purpose of this technique is to elicit negative information. Another reason interviewers use this approach is to see if you can respond appropriately when you are subjected to pressure. If you are applying for a job that requires you to function under pressure, you may encounter some of the following common stress-interviewing techniques:

- Blindside—An innocuous question followed by one that raises your anxiety level. "What is the best job you ever had?" followed by "Have you ever been fired, and if yes, why?" or "What was the worst job you ever held and why?"

- Serial questions posed in rapid fire order. "Why are you coming back to work at this time?" "What part of retirement bothers you the most?" "Explain why you retired in the first place." "What was the worst part of your last job?"

- Invitations to provide negative information about yourself. "What is your worst personality trait?"

- Rudeness. "That's really a stupid idea, isn't it? That wouldn't work in our company."

- Establish time limits. "In one minute, tell me why you are qualified for this job." The interviewer looks at his or her watch while you are talking.

- Interviewer keeps pushing your weaknesses. "You mentioned that at times you are overly conservative. Give me an example." Interviewee responds. "That sounds more like shortsightedness to me." Interviewee responds. "Seems like your conservative approach may hurt your ability to function at times.

- Interviewer challenges what you term as strength or challenges your technical expertise. "You say that you are a hard worker, and you have always spent many hours on the job. Maybe it is because you aren't as efficient as other people."

- Interviewer interrupts unexpectedly when you are doing well and switches topics. "Okay, that's enough about how you handled that. Tell me what you would do if you didn't like your boss."

- Puts interviewee on the spot. "What do you think of me as an interviewer?"

Note that each of these techniques is designed to elicit negative information about you personally or the way you function on the job. These, in the vernacular of many, are land mines. However, they are also a great opportunity for you to show your maturity by being coolheaded and not playing the game.

Responding to the stress interview.   First and foremost, recognize what is going on. Interviewers do not invite job candidates in for tea and crumpets. Also, they don't invite them in to make them feel bad. They are simply doing what they were hired to do: determine if you can do the job. If you leave an interview feeling bad about the way you were treated, you probably misperceived what was happening. If the interviewer's nonverbal behavior or verbal behavior changes, the interviewer has changed strategies. Just tell yourself, "Here we go. This is my chance to get this job." Give the interviewer a big smile and proceed.

Our instincts tell us to respond to stressful situations by withdrawing nonverbally. You can do this by breaking off eye contact, increasing the interpersonal space between yourself and the interviewer by either turning your torso or leaning back, or by fidgeting, usually by moving your hands or swinging your feet. Be aware of and avoid these tendencies to withdraw.

It is always a good strategy when answering stressful questions to use the technique taught in beginning speech classes, that is, repeat the question before answering it. This allows you to fully understand what is being asked and to compose your answer. It puts you in control. This is the recognize-reflect-respond technique that is used not only in speech classes but by trainers who help politicians and others learn to respond to stressful reporters' interviews. You may not want to literally repeat every question, because that becomes boring and seems a bit stilted to your listener. You may want to use some of the following strategies instead.

Interviewer: "What were the worst things about your last job?" (Interviewer is trying to see if applicant will complain.)

Interviewee: "Let me see. The worst aspects of my last job? Well, "worst" is relative, and I don't want to make it sound as though I was in a terrible situation, because I wasn't. Really, the only negative aspect of the job for me was that I had been with the company for 20 years, and I had stopped growing. I just wasn't making the contribution I am capable of making." (Interviewee identifies a legitimate reason for leaving without denigrating company or supervisors. Also identifies a personal strength: a desire to contribute.)

Interviewer: "Why did you suddenly retire and then suddenly decide to go back to work?" (Interviewer is suggesting impulsiveness.)

Interviewee: "I'm sure that these changes seem sudden, and perhaps that is because I haven't communicated what has occurred clearly enough. I planned to retire for 10 years prior to taking the plunge into retirement, so it really wasn't that sudden. My wife and I had planned everything, except how I miss the stimulation of working. We have fully discussed my returning to work. I knew when I retired that I was still capable of making a contribution, and that is what I want to do for your company by taking the job we are discussing." (Interviewee demonstrates an ability to plan.)

Interviewer One: "What would you do the first week on the job?"

Interviewer Two: "While you are answering that, think about the problems you would expect to encounter if you come aboard."

Interviewer Three: "Also, tell us how you expect to handle the stress in this job." (Interviewers are trying to determine how interviewee responds to stress.)

Interviewee: "Let's see if I can sort these questions out. The first week on the job, the problems I would expect, and how I would handle the stress. I'll start with the easiest one first. I handle stress by solving problems as they come up so that stress doesn't accumulate and by maintaining a positive work environment. When people support each other, stress is much less of a problem on the job. The other two problems are related in a sense. I've been told what the problems are. For example, I've been told that there is a morale problem. But I like to keep an open mind. My first week on the job and probably several weeks after that would be to identify the specific problems that have arisen and begin to develop solutions to those problems." (Interviewee demonstrates ability to field multiple questions, openness, and sets self up as a problem solver.)

Finally, do use the recognize-reflect-respond technique to help you respond to stressful questions. Do not avoid questions, and if you feel that you may have missed a portion of the question because of your anxiety, it is permissible to ask the interviewer to repeat the question. Just don't do it too often.

The end of the interview

Long ago, psychologists established the principles of recency and primacy. We tend to remember the first and last things we experience in an event. Your interviewer is going to complete her or his rating of you soon after the interview is complete. For this reason, the last few moments in an interview are critical. End each interview by:

- Thanking the interviewer

- Restating that you can do the job well

- Offering to provide any additional information

- Asking for the job

- Asking when a decision will be made

Of these steps, none is more important than asking for the job. Typically a statement such as the following will suffice.

Interviewee: "I've enjoyed talking to you about the vacancy you have, and I want to restate that I can do the job and do it well. I am very interested in the job, and I hope you will offer it to me. Has a deadline been established for filling the job?"

There is a fine line between appearing interested and enthusiastic and looking desperate. Don't cross that line. Although I am not exactly sure why this is the case, people are suspicious of those who appear to be desperate, perhaps because they feel they may not have been entirely honest in the interview process.

A different type of problem   One of the dilemmas that some interviewees face is that they go into an interview with a job offer in hand that expires in a few days, and the interviewer tells them that it is going to be two weeks before a decision is made. If you are in this situation and you are more interested in the job for which you are interviewing than the one that has been offered, you have three choices: (1) Try to get the deadline for accepting or rejecting the job that has been offered postponed. (2) Tell the interviewer that you have to know sooner because you have another offer. In this case, you need to identify the source of this offer and the deadline. (3) Run the risk of not getting either job. Since the third option is rarely acceptable, the first and second are your only alternatives.

If you feel that the deadline that has been established cannot be changed, tell the interviewer about the offer. In many instances, the deadline date for filling the job can be changed, particularly if you are one of the leading candidates. If you are unsure whether the deadline can be changed, wait until you return home, call the company that has made the offer, and ask that the deadline be extended. If they are unwilling to change the deadline for your response, then call the interviewer and explain your situation.

Post-interview   Upon returning home, immediately write a note to the interviewer that thanks him or her for the opportunity to interview and restates your interest in the job. This should be on formal stationery (white, buff, or gray) and should be typed. A note such as the following will suffice.

Ms. Jane Q. Interviewer
Personnel Director
XYZ Corporation
Someplace, NY 00045

Dear Ms. Interviewer:

I want to thank you for the opportunity to interview for the position of sales manager at XYZ corporation. My initial research suggested that your company presents an excellent opportunity for me, and the information I gained from you confirmed that research. I want to take this opportunity to restate my interest in the position and reaffirm my conviction that I can do an excellent job for your company.

Again, thank you for the opportunity to interview. I'm looking forward to hearing from you.

Sincerely,

Jay P. Interviewee

Summary

In this chapter I have provided a basic overview of the interview, starting with preparation and ending in post-interview procedures. Preparation is the most essential aspect of the interview, because if you are properly prepared, you will be confident about your ability to respond to questions. However, you must translate this confidence into communication that you can do the job and do it better than other people. I could overwhelm you with dozens of other suggestions about how to handle your nonverbal behavior in the interview, but research shows that too many positives can result in a negative: you can look so slick that you seem like a wind-up doll, not a real person. Just smile, maintain eye contact, and relax.

The next chapter deals almost entirely with a topic that was touched on in this chapter: answering tough questions. I have recommended that you, as an older worker, make an extra effort to dress well, get in shape, and preempt questions about your health. As a mature worker, you have many assets that are marketable, but the truth is that you often have some barriers to overcome. If you answer the tough questions well, you will be a success in the job hunt.

Answering the Tough Questions, Asking Some of Your Own, And Closing the Deal

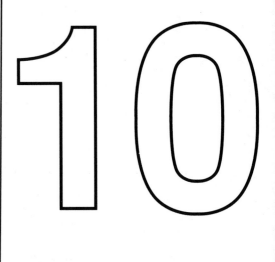

Did you know that the interviewer comes into the interview with a positive or negative bias, depending upon your paper credentials?

Last Chance   The interview constitutes your last chance to market yourself to the interviewer. The interviewer has already reviewed your paper credentials, including your resume, recommendations, and transcripts, if appropriate. On the basis of that review, he or she has developed a bias, a preconceived notion about your suitability in relationship to the other people who are to be interviewed. The purpose of the interview is to confirm the bias. By never letting him or her see you sweat, you can offset a negative bias and confirm a positive bias. This is your last chance for employment in this job.

Tell The Truth

Earlier, during the discussion of resume preparation, you were reminded that falsifying information on a resume constitutes fraud and can lead to your dismissal long after you are hired. The same principle applies to the interview. The moral? Tell the truth. Telling the truth means do not embellish, distort, withhold, or otherwise alter information when you answer questions. If an interviewer asks, "Were you ever dismissed from a job?", you must answer "yes" if that is the case. However, answering "yes" does not prevent you from turning this request for negative information into a positive. People who are successful turn negatives into positives.

When It Is None Of Their Business: The Illegal Question

Legally, interviewers cannot base hiring decisions on age, race, religion, country of origin, marital status, whether you intend to have children, or political affiliations. This does not mean that discrimination against women, minorities, older workers, and people with various political beliefs does not exist, and there will be times when interviewers will ask questions designed to illicit this type of information. Some people have unwittingly disqualified themselves from jobs by volunteering information about themselves. Never tell the interviewer your religious or political affiliation, your marital status and your plans to have children, your age, or your nationality.

But what if they ask? If you are asked illegal questions, you have a decision to make. Do you refuse and tell the interviewer that you believe this is an improper question and in all probability lose the job, or do you answer and run the risk of losing the job? Most job seekers opt for the latter. It may be a good idea to remember, should you be confronted with this situation, that you can file suit later if it seems that discrimination played a role in the hiring process. However, as an older worker, it is not likely that you will encounter questions that are obviously illegal. What is more likely is that you will be asked questions that indirectly get at age. These present you with a golden opportunity to turn questions that are fishing for negative information into positives.

Retired Workers' Advantages

Enough of this discussion about discrimination. Let's begin generally to prepare your case as a retired worker and then get into the answers of specific questions, including those aimed at eliciting negative information. I have prepared a list of advantages that you have that make you superior to younger workers. See if you can add to this list by thinking about your own strengths.

Advantages of older workers

- Often more stable marital relationships, which allows them to focus their energies on the job.

- Pressure of child rearing nearly complete or behind them.

- Experience in dealing with life situations—maturity.

- Less oriented to money and can withstand the ups and downs of jobs with uncertain financial conditions without the stress experienced by younger workers.

- Working because they choose to, not because they have to.

- Depending on age, may not work long enough for the company to be vested in the retirement program, and thus hiring older workers reduces the company's overall financial obligation.

- More stable financially.

- More work experience.

- Can focus on the job at hand. Don't have to worry about climbing the corporate ladder.

- Greater loyalty. Turnover is reduced.

Turning Positives To Negatives

Memorize the advantages of the older worker. Add your own advantages to this list. Then memorize how your training and experience allow you to do the job for which you are applying. Once you are in the interview, take every opportunity to tell why you will do the job well and the advantages you bring to the workplace. If there is a question about your work experience, give a complete description of what you have done and tell why that experience makes you qualified to do the job. If you are asked a sly question that relates to your age such as, "We are looking for a person with a high level of energy to do this job. How would you rate yourself on this dimension?", answer the question and then tell about your advantages. Turn a request for a negative into a positive. In order to do this you must R-R-R, recognize (what is being asked), reflect (think how to turn negatives to positives), and respond (actually turn requests for negative information or positive information into positive statements about yourself). If you are asked about an obvious weakness, admit that on paper you may not appear as qualified as some others, then construct a positive answer based upon your advantages and your age. Turning negatives to positives is your key to successful interviewing. If the interviewer (in exasperation) asks if you always answer questions by turning negatives into positives, respond that this is not always the case, but basically you believe in yourself and you are sure you can do the job (and you turned the negative to a positive).

Sixteen Ways To Commit Suicide During The Interview

In the foregoing section I told you how to succeed at interviewing. Now I'm going to give you 16 ways to make absolutely certain you never work unless you are the only applicant.

1. Don't prepare. Make sure you know nothing about the job or the company. This will certainly work if you ask the interviewer's name and company.

2. Be late, then don't apologize.

3. Dress badly. No belt, a two-inch tie, and frayed cuffs should suffice, particularly if your clothes are wrinkled.

4. Get defensive when you are asked a tough question. Cave in to pressure. Start your answer with "That's unfair, and it makes me upset just to think about it."

5. Be a know-it-all. Correct the interviewer at least twice. Be unrelentingly argumentative throughout.

6. Don't smile. Be as glum as possible. It may help you to remember that cheerfulness is a sign of a sick mind.

7. Talk in a monotone voice. Generally, don't appear to be too excited. This technique works best if you act like excitement might bring on a heart attack.

8. Appear uncertain about the job. Act like you are shopping for opportunity. Statements like "I'm not sure this job and company are right for me," are sure to impress.

9. Make it clear that your hobby comes before work. Interviewers are always impressed with people who know how to fill their time.

10. Suggest that you aren't what you used to be. Point out as many aches and pains as possible to support your point.

11. Complain about how badly you were treated on your last job. Better yet, complain that things aren't what they used to be.

12. Talk about your funeral arrangements. The interviewer is bound to be impressed with how forward-looking you are.

13. Criticize the president and at least one senator. Maybe you will step on one or more of the interviewer's toes.

14. Be self-effacing. When complimented, say, "Aw shucks, I've just been lucky."

15. Be racist or sexist. This approach works best when the interviewer is a woman or a member of a minority group.

16. Be sure that the interviewer knows that you are a feminist, that you hate feminists, or that you take strong stands on issues such as abortion.

Okay, enough sarcasm, but hopefully you get the idea. If you really intend to self-destruct during the interview, save yourself and the interviewer a lot of trouble and stay home.

The Tough Questions And Some Answers That Will Work—Can You Really Do The Job?

These questions come in many forms, but their purpose is to see if you will be able to perform the tasks set forth in the job description. This is particularly true when interviewers are looking at a retired worker's potential. Some questions follow. After the questions and some sample answers, a space is provided for you to write your own answers.

Q1. *You have applied for a job as a(n) _____. Tell me about your qualifications for this job.* (Invitation to show off your knowledge and confidence in your ability.)
A. Let me begin by talking about the job as it has been described to me. As I understand it, you want someone who can . . . (Spell out in as much detail as possible. The interviewer may add some details.) Now let me review some of my experiences and accomplishments. (Go systematically through how your experience and accomplishments will allow you to perform the job at hand. Emphasize your accomplishments. Interviewers want evidence of accomplishments. Experience is secondary.)

Write your answer to question 1 here: _____

_____

_____

_____

_____

Q2. *It seems to me that you are a bit weak in [some aspect of the job]. How would you compensate for this weakness?.* (This is the old "When-did-you-stop-beating-your-wife?" question. The interviewer expects you to reveal that you really do have some weaknesses.)
A. I'm not sure that I agree with your assessment that I have a weakness in [the area specified]. Let me point out some of my background and accomplishments in this particular area.
A. If you do have identified weakness: I admit that I do have some weaknesses, but these are more than offset by my strengths. More importantly, I don't see them as a barrier to my performance in the job. It does mean that I have to hit the ground running (action), learn what I need to know by . . . (suggest concrete strategy

for overcoming weakness), and then move ahead. Let me tell you what happened when I was faced with a similar situation in the past. (Tell of your accomplishments in overcoming weaknesses in the past with concrete examples.)

Write your answer to question 2 here: _____

_____

_____

_____

_____

Q3. *How has your experience prepared you to perform this particular job?* (Here is an invitation to talk about what lessons you have learned in your work life that will help you on this job.)
A. I've learned that every company works a little differently, and it is important that you learn the system. (You are a team player.)

I've also learned that people must work together to maximize success. (You are collaborative.)

I've learned what a lot of others have learned. There is no substitute for careful planning, which results in carefully conceived goals, a carefully orchestrated plan to accomplish those goals, and hard work. I've also learned that at times there is a need to take carefully calculated risks. (Portrays you as a hard worker who plans, who is willing to take a few risks. You will undoubtedly get a follow-up question to the risk-taking part of your answer, so you need to be prepared to explain your definition of a calculated risk and when you would decide to take one.)

For example, when I was with X Construction Company, we were behind on a high-visibility project. I decided that it would be better to pay some overtime and cut into our profits than to finish several months behind schedule and suffer as a result of the bad publicity. We made money on the project, and because it was so well received, we got three similar jobs.

Or you might answer:

I was assigned to a territory that had been fairly unproductive for the company. The word from the people who had been in that territory before was that a "good-old-boy" face-to-face approach was the only thing that would work, but that was a problem because of the size of the territory. I designed a systematic approach that involved periodic telephone calls, weekly faxes, and one-third less face-to-face contacts and piloted it with a few of our customers. It increased sales by 20 percent in the pilot group and eventually increased sales by 18 percent for the territory. Because our costs were lower, the net gain was 22 percent. (Highlights your accomplishments and illustrates that you are willing to take risks.)

Write your answer to question 3 here: _____

_____

_____

_____

Q4. *Why are you willing to accept a job for which you are obviously overqualified?* (This is a request for negative information. Interviewers tend to believe that people who are highly qualified or have a lot of experience in an area will be bored with a similar job.)
A. It is true that I have done similar jobs in the past, but I see this job as a clear challenge to use what I have learned in a new environment. In my view, this is a win–win situation. I win because I will be doing something that I can really be enthusiastic about. Your company wins because it can take advantage of the expertise I have developed. Besides, it is hard for me to imagine a situation where I would be too well prepared. (Portrays yourself as enthusiastic and points out benefits to company.)

Write your answer to question 4 here: _____

_____

_____

_____

Q5. *Have you ever been fired?* (If yes, this is a stressful question aimed at getting your reaction. It is an invitation to complain and blame others.)

A. Yes, I have. (Give the reason, then explain what you learned from the experience.) I was fired early in my career because of low productivity. What I learned from that was that companies need their employees to contribute, and I have been a top producer ever since. (Portrays you as honest and a person who changes with feedback—not a blamer.)

Write your answer to question 5 here: _____

_____

_____

_____

_____

What Kind Of Person Are You, Anyway?

These questions are just as important as the questions about your job qualifications. Interviewers want workers that match the corporate culture and that can get along with others on the job.

Q1. *What are your greatest strengths?* (This is an invitation to brag, but remember that this question is likely to be followed by a probe regarding your weaknesses. It may also be followed by a challenge to your beliefs about your strengths in stress interviews. However, this is not a time to be shy about listing your strengths, but in doing so, keep in mind what the job requires.)

A. My greatest strength is that I am a problem solver. In my previous jobs I have . . . (list concrete examples of accomplishments). Perhaps just as importantly, I can get things done while maintaining harmony in the workplace. The way I do this is by resolving personal differences when they arise. (Tell a story about how you did this.) I work well with superiors and subordinates. I try to be sensitive to the needs of the people who work with me, but I have high expectations of their performance, just as I have high expectations of myself. I think people who have worked under me would describe me as demanding but fair. (Give points that the interviewer will be concerned about.)

Or you might answer:

Perhaps my greatest strength is my ability to communicate. I have found that I can be quite persuasive if the need arises and that I can communicate in unambiguous terms. This helps me in my relationships on the job. I am also a good problem solver, partially because I can identify problems and communicate them clearly to others. (Identifies an essential skill.)

Or you might answer:

My greatest strength is my concern for others. I have found that when you care about the people you work with and communicate that caring by respecting people, things run more smoothly. The result is that I believe that I have been able to inspire loyalty, and when problems need to be solved, the people I work with pull together to get the job done. (Finish by telling a story to illustrate your point.) (Portrays you as a concerned problem solver.)

Write your answer to question 1 here: _____

_____

_____

_____

_____

Q2. *What are your greatest weaknesses?* (Clearly a request for negative information. Turn the request into a positive.)
A. I don't believe that I have any weaknesses when it comes to being successful on this job. There are certainly times when I work too hard, but when a project is

completed, I can pull back and recharge my batteries. I may also be a bit of a perfectionist, but the result of that is a little more stress for me and a better job for the company. (You have turned a request for negative information into a positive portrayal of yourself.)

Write your answer to question 2 here: _____

_____

_____

_____

_____

Q3. *This job requires a lot of energy. How would you rate your energy level?* (This is a request for you to tip your hand about your age.)
A. I have a very high energy level. Having the energy to function at a high level has never been a problem for me. (Simply disputes supposition of interviewer. This will be a better answer if you give an example to illustrate your point.)

Or you might answer:

I'm quite capable of working long hours when the need arises. Energy has never been a problem. I've also found that I have gotten more efficient as I have gained more experience. (Portrays yourself as having high energy and lists one of the advantages of the more mature worker.)

Write your answer to question 3 here: _____

_____

_____

_____

_____

Q4. *How long do you expect to work?* (This is a question that is also age related. Your circumstances will dictate the answer. However, unless you are interviewing for a time-limited job, many companies will not be interested in employees that expect to work very short periods of time.)

A. As long as I can make a contribution and the company believes I'm doing a good job. (Provides a picture of you as desiring to be a contributor.)

Or you might answer:

I'm projecting 10 years. However, I'm really excited about the opportunity that the job presents, and so this could change. (Portrays you with definite goals, but as enthusiastic about the job.)

Write your answer to question 4 here: _____

_____

_____

Q5. *How do you respond to pressure on the job?* (This is a request for negative information that provides you with an opportunity to highlight your strengths.)

A. I think the greater the pressure, the better I respond. (Then tell a story to illustrate your point.)

Or you might answer:

I'm like most people. I feel the pressure, but over time I've developed ways of coping with it. I exercise regularly, which I find helps. I also take a few minutes each day to do some relaxation exercises. (Shows you as human, makes point that you exercise, and shows your maturity.)

Write your answer to question 5 here: _____

_____

_____

Q6. *What are your biggest accomplishments?* (This is a question designed to determine your work values. Most interviewers want to eliminate workers that are primarily oriented to money.)

A. Two accomplishments stand out in my mind. Before retiring, I was the leading sales producer for my company seven out of the last ten years, and I was second the three years I wasn't first. I miss the competition. Second, I helped a young sales person who was struggling a bit really turn his approach around. I enjoyed that brief mentoring process. It made me feel good when he moved into the top-10 list of producers. (Portrays you as achievement oriented and competitive, but not to the extent that you are unwilling to help others.)

Write your answer to question 6 here: _____

_____

_____

_____

_____

Q7. *What aspects of this job are least interesting to you?* (Trying to get at values and sources of motivation. Also trying to determine whether most important aspects of job are of greatest interest.)

A. The most important aspects of the job are the things I'm most interested in. These are . . . (list). However, I'm not excited about writing the monthly reports and other routine dimensions of the job. The way I handle things like that is to get them done immediately so they won't be hanging over my head. That allows me to derive more enjoyment from the parts of the job I enjoy the most. (Depicts you as punctual and willing to do the things you don't enjoy.)

Write your answer to question 7 here: _____

_____

_____

_____

_____

Q8. *What were the strengths and weaknesses of your last boss or company?* (This is an invitation to self-destruct by complaining about your last boss or work situation. The answer will be determined by how you viewed your last boss. Obviously if you admired her or him, this poses no problem.)
A. (Interviewee didn't like boss.) I believe that her strengths were that she was well organized, had good interpersonal skills, and had reasonably high standards. Her weaknesses were that she didn't always follow through on promises and was sometimes indecisive. (Unless you are urged to do so, do not embellish these points. If you are asked to give examples, make them succinct and factual.)

Write your answer to question 8 here: _____

_____

_____

_____

_____

Q9. *What is your supervisory style?* (Interviewer is trying to determine if you will fit into corporate culture.)
A. My style is to lay out clear expectations and then let the employee use his or her skills to meet those expectations. However, I ask for regular progress reports so I can keep abreast of projects. I also try to be positive, even for little things. People need to know when they do well. (Depicts you as task oriented, clear communicator, positive, and in control.)

Or you might answer:

I work with employees to lay out objectives, and then we develop plans to accomplish these objectives. I like to have people who work with me choose the parts of the project they want to work on once the tasks are clear. I hold regular staff meetings to assess progress (portrays you as a collaborative superior who works with employees).

Write your answer to question 9 here: _____

_____

_____

_____

Q10. *You'll be working with a number of people who are more highly educated than yourself. How do you feel about that?* (Interviewer wants to know if you are intimidated by educated people.)

A. I think education is very important, and working with people who are well educated should be stimulating because it will give me the opportunity to keep growing. I have a long track record of outstanding job performance, and I know that I can continue that with your company. I also expect to learn things from the people I work with, so I'm looking forward to interacting with the people you mention. (Portrays you as confident but open to learning from those around you).

Write your answer to question 10 here: _____

_____

_____

_____

Q11. *Your supervisor is likely to be much younger than you are and have somewhat less experience. How do you feel about that?* (Interviewer wants to know if you will resent a younger person.)

A. The age of my supervisor is of no concern. I have learned to establish collaborative relationships with people of all ages in my career. (Depicts you as open-minded and points to your experience.)

Write your answer to question 11 here: _____

_____

_____

_____

Q12. *What would you do if you didn't like your supervisor?* (Stress question asking for negative information.)
A. First, it would be an unusual situation. In my career I have had to cope with numerous supervisors, and I have managed to do well. But, if I really did not like my supervisor, I would try to make very certain that it did not influence my job performance. If I thought that there were something in our relationship that could be fixed, I would initiate a discussion with the supervisor to determine the cause of the problem and see if it could be remedied. (Points to the advantages of your experience, affirms your high standards, and shows you as willing to work on solutions to problems.)

Write your answer to question 12 here: _____

_____

_____

_____

_____

_____

Q13. *Don't you ever get angry?* (A request for negative information posed in a stressful manner.)
A. Of course I do, but I have learned that blowing up only makes things worse. I try to channel my anger into solving the problem. (Tell a story about when you did this.) (Portrays you as an experienced, mature person who can cope with negative emotions.)

Write your answer to question 13 here: _____

_____

_____

_____

_____

Can We Make A Deal?

During the interview, the interviewer may decide to either make an offer or determine what type of offer is going to be necessary to hire you. If this is the case, the nature of the questions may change to focus on salary, working conditions, job title, fringe benefits, and other relevant factors. Of these factors, no negotiation is more important than the one dealing with salary. The employer typically has a salary range. Potential employees have minimum salary expectations that will allow them to be satisfied on the job and high-end salary aspirations. It is these two ranges that must be meshed if the deal is to be consummated. The following questions address salary and other factors that must be settled before the job offer.

Q1. *What other jobs have you applied for?* (Interviewer wants to know what the competition is.)
A. I have applied to X, Y, and Z; or, I haven't applied to any other jobs. (Tells interviewer your status.)

Write your answer to question 1 here: _____

_____

_____

Q2. *Would you relocate if necessary?* (Trying to get at your motivation and flexibility, not necessarily an indication of the company plan to relocate you. If you won't move, the job is not high priority.)
A. I'm willing to move if necessary; or, I'm not. (Again, lets interviewer know your status.)

Write your answer to question 2 here: _____

_____

_____

Q3. *What did you earn on your last job?* (Potentially a double-barreled question. If your salary was high on your last job and you are applying for a lower-paying job, which is frequently the case, you can scare off an interviewer because he or she may believe that you will be unhappy with a lower-paying job. On the other hand, if you are applying for a higher-paying job, your low salary in your previous job may lower the final offer.)
A. My salary was $42,000, but I'm not sure that is relevant to this job. Explain why it isn't relevant.) (Tells interviewer that some negotiation is necessary.)

Or you might answer:

I made $42,000 the last year I worked for X Corporation. I would expect that the salary is probably a bit lower (higher) on this job. (A signal that you have done your homework and have developed some expectations about salary.)

Write your answer to question 3 here: _____

_____

_____

_____

_____

Q4. *What do you believe you're worth?* (This is a request for negative information as well as an attempt by the interviewer to get an inkling about your salary expectations. If you have an overinflated view of your worth, you won't get the job.)
A. My worth should be determined by two variables. Initially, it should be based on my potential to do the job and the salaries others in the same position are paid if our credentials are equivalent. After that, it should be based on my performance. (Communicates that you want to be paid the same as others doing the same job, and you are not afraid of merit reviews.)

Write your answer to question 4 here: _____

_____

_____

_____

_____

Q5. *What salary will it take to have you come aboard?* (It's show time. When this question is asked, you need to make your salary demands known).

A. I believe $35,000 would be an equitable salary, but fringe benefits other than salary are important as well. What is the nature of the benefits package? (Leaves salary open and continues negotiation.)

Write your answer to question 5 here: _____

_____

_____

Q6. *We had budgeted a bit less. I'm authorized to offer you $32,000. Will you be willing to accept this amount?* (This is really the crunch, but feel free to continue the negotiation. They want you, or they wouldn't have come this far.)
A. We are pretty close. I'd appreciate it if you would try to get a bit more money. I think I deserve $35,000 for . . . (specify reasons). (This answer allows you to keep your options open, including accepting the offer.)

Write your answer to question 6 here: _____

_____

_____

More About Tough Questions

Interviewers may ask dozens of tough questions, but they fall into the previous three categories: Can you do the job?, What kind of person are you and will you fit into our company?, and Can we close the deal? The following are more examples of tough questions that you can use for practice. When constructing your answers, remember: recognize, reflect, and respond.

Questions about your qualifications

• What qualifications do you possess that others we might interview will not?

• Why will you be successful in this particular job?

• Are you looking for a permanent job?

• What are your personal characteristics that will be most useful on this job?

- We need to increase productivity. If you are given the job, what would you do to solve this problem?

- Give us some details about your technical competence.

- Prove to me that you can successfully fill this job.

- If you were the interviewer, what would you want to know about your qualifications?

- What is the biggest challenge posed by this job, and which of your credentials qualifies you to handle that challenge?

- Which of your qualifications would you have to improve to be successful?

Questions about personal traits

- What will you do if someone really chews you out?

- When thinking about this job, what seems most important: the power, the prestige, or the salary?

- Tell me about your decision-making style.

- Is your decision-making style always the same, regardless of the circumstances?

- What have people told you is your worst trait?

- What if your boss were a woman? Man? Minority?

- Tell me about a time when your life changed dramatically, and describe how you adjusted to the change.

- Do you prefer to work alone or with people?

- How do you handle rejection?

- What kind of money manager are you in your personal life?

- How do you resolve interpersonal disputes?

- What is the biggest problem in your life right now?

Questions about closing the deal

- What has been your salary history?

- Would you have worked for less on your last job?

- Will you expect a promotion?

- Why did it take you so long to decide you wanted to try a retirement career?

- Are you willing to submit to a physical examination?

- Are you willing to take a drug test?

- Are you willing to take a battery of psychological examinations to help us better assess your potential for this job?

- What kind of benefits are you expecting if you are hired?

- How would you respond if I offered you the job but told you that the first three months you are going to be on probation?

- We have flex-time employee scheduling. Because you would be a new employee, you would be at the bottom of the list in terms of choosing your schedule. How do you feel about that?

Asking Your Own Questions

One of the reasons people flunk the employment interview is that they do not ask any questions when they are given the opportunity to do so. At least once in each interview, the interviewer will put the ball in your court simply by saying, "Do you have any questions?" Failure to ask questions may be viewed as lack of interest, failure to prepare for the interview, or lack of assertiveness. It will not be viewed as a positive factor, so ask questions.

Asking questions provides you with an opportunity to show how well you have prepared for the interview and how enthusiastic you are about the job. Listed below are some typical questions that interviewees ask. Each of these questions is posed in a manner that says something positive about you, that may allow you to say something positive about the company, and should elicit a positive response from the interviewer. Since interviewers also have the role of recruiting employees, they will be positive unless you ask a question that forces them to be negative.

This is not to suggest that interviewers will be dishonest. It only means that they will try to be as positive as possible. Your best chances of being hired are when the tone of the interview is positive. Prior to going to your interview, you need to write down some of your own questions that use the positive–positive format.

About the company

- I noticed that the company's stock has been going up recently. That is exciting, because it usually means that something positive in the way of sales or product development is in the works. What is the company doing to warrant the increase in stock prices? (Shows you did your homework, that you are excited by what you found, and invites interviewer to make a positive statement.)

- Tell me about the company's performance review process. I know that some people are concerned about being evaluated, but I like to get feedback about my work, so I'm wondering how often it occurs and who does it? (Shows excitement, that you are aware of the need for performance appraisal, and invites interviewer to discuss those aspects of his or her company.)

- How would you characterize the culture of the organization? My research suggests that the organization is fairly formal and that people are expected to operate within the organizational structure. I'm most comfortable in those types of situations, so I'm hoping you can confirm that for me. (Shows that you did research, that you are willing to fit in to culture, and invites the interviewer to comment and confirm. Incidently, you'd better be right.)

- Security is not an overriding issue for me, but I'm wondering when I would achieve exempt status. (Depicts one of your traits, illustrates that you understand that you will likely begin nonexempt role, and invites interviewer to confirm.)

- I'm flexible, but I am curious about the decision-making style of the senior-level managers. Would you characterize their styles as more autocratic or democratic? (Illustrates one of your important traits, shows interest beyond routine aspects of the job, and invites the interviewer to discuss an important aspect of the company.)

• Many corporations are going through restructuring at this time, and while the ratings on the financial health of your company look very good, I'm wondering if restructuring is planned in the near future. (Shows that you have done your homework and invites positive response.)

About the job

• As you consider the overall scheme of things, how would you relate the importance of this job to the company (or to the division)? My own analysis suggests that it is quite important, and I'm pleased, because I like to be in the thick of things because I believe I can make a difference. (Depicts you as confident and invites interviewer to make positive statement about job/company.)

• I believe that I have a good understanding of the job, but could you describe what I will be doing from your perspective? (Illustrates that you have drawn conclusions and asks interviewer to make positive comments about job.)

• One area where I have little information is about the people I will be working with. I'm wondering if you can describe them for me. (Shows that you are concerned about the work environment and invited interviewer to describe the people.)

• I have been able to deal with a wide variety of people in my career, but I am curious about how you do see me fitting into this group. (Shows confidence and interest in meshing harmoniously and places interviewer in position of positively evaluating you.)

• I'm positive that I can fill the job, but I'm wondering about what specific contributions I would be expected to make. (Shows confidence and concern about contributing and forces interviewer to lay out major roles. You should affirm with head nods and then verbally that you can do a good job.)

• Which of my skills would be needed most on the job? (Again shows concern about contributing and asks interviewer to evaluate you positively.)

• I have found that I can deal with many types of situations, but can you project changes that may occur in this job over the next five years? (Shows flexibility and asks interviewer to discuss positive changes.)

Other questions you might ask

- I want to keep growing personally and professionally. What opportunities does your company provide for personal and professional growth?

- I want to make a contribution. What are the strengths and weaknesses of the team with which I will be working?

- Assuming that I do a good job, will I have opportunities to become involved in other areas of the company?

- What is the most exciting thing going on in the company right now? Will I be connected to it in any way?

- My research shows that X, Y, and Z are your biggest competitors. How do you see the company competing with these and other companies in the future?

- Do you see the culture of the organization changing? I know that many companies are going to flat organizations that allow greater freedom and require employees to accept more responsibility.

- Historically the company's market niche has been with young adults. Given the aging of America, will the company be developing products to compete in this market?

- Technology plays an important role in the job I am seeking. How has the work group utilized technology to increase effectiveness and efficiency?

- I'm an exercise buff. Does the company provide exercise facilities?

- I'm naturally curious about all aspects of the company I work for. How does the company keep people informed about things that are happening within the company?

- I'm excited about this job, but I'm also interested in advancement after I have demonstrated what I can do. How are jobs posted in the company?

- I enjoy learning from others. Is there a mentoring program?

Closing The Deal Your thinking about salary should begin the moment you start thinking about a job. Essentially, there are three sources of information about salary:

- company insiders

- the *Occupational Outlook Handbook* (OOH)

- publications available from your employment security office or State Occupational Information Coordinating Committee (SOICC)

The OOH information provides ranges of monetary compensation for particular jobs and can be useful as you begin to establish expectations. Local labor market information, such as that available from your local employment office or SOICC (call your department of labor for the telephone number), can help you narrow your expectations. This information is developed for your state and may not be entirely applicable to companies that have offices throughout the country. Inside information is, of course, the best information about salary, but this may be difficult to access unless you have a friend or acquaintance in the company.

Another way to think about salary is to consider your needs along with your own estimate of your worth. There are several ways to be unhappy on the job, but doing a job for less money than others is one of the most certain ways. When people work for considerably less than they think they are worth, they are also likely to be unhappy. However, many workers who have been retired earlier have found it necessary to accept jobs at salaries one-third less than they were earning in their previous jobs. In considering what you are worth, you may need to adjust your expectations based on some realistic labor market considerations.

As every worker knows, salary is only one part of compensation. Profit-sharing plans and stock options can increase monetary compensation. For a retired worker, fringe benefits in the form of medical and dental care packages, tax shelters, life insurance policies, short- and long-term disability policies, personal leave policies, sick days, educational benefits, leisure opportunities, vacation time, and retirement benefits may be more important than salary. You will certainly want to determine the extent to which travel expenses are reimbursed, including allowances for meals and hotel rooms. Some companies have flat rates for mileage, meals, and hotels that do not cover actual costs.

Ultimately you need to arrive at a minimum compensation package you would expect in order to accept the job. The interviewer has a maximum that he or she can offer. Obviously if the maximum is lower than the minimum you expect, you have certain problems.

In most situations, the maximums established by companies, governmental agencies, hospitals, and many other agencies is based upon the job classification. That is, employers have jobs classified by the amount of responsibility, required experience and education needed to fill that job. If your minimum and the interviewer's maximum don't mesh, you should ask if the job can be reclassified to the next higher level. This has the advantages of increasing your entry salary and your future salary, because the cap on a job with a higher classification is also higher. Remember, one of the best predictors of future salary in many organizations is entry salary.

If you cannot reach immediate agreement on the entry-level salary, another negotiation ploy is to talk about future compensation. In some instances, employers will agree to three- or six-month raises, contingent on performance. If the employer is unwilling to meet your minimum salary requirements, negotiations should be terminated.

Obviously you do not wish to enter compensation negotiations seeking the minimum. If you are asked how much salary it will take, and you have been unable to get inside information, you may need to ask the interviewer, "How much do other people earn doing the same or a similar job within the company?" This is a legitimate question, and since the interviewer's job switches from screening to recruiting once you express an interest, you should get a reasonable, although often cagey, answer. In the situation where the range of salaries given by the interviewer is less than your minimum, you face a dilemma: should you go for the top, middle, or lower ranges? This depends on your assessment of how you stack up against other people in similar positions. This is not a time to be timid. If you make a totally unrealistic request, an interviewer may withdraw the offer. Begin by asking what you think is the maximum the company will pay. If they are unwilling or unable to meet your request, they will typically make a counteroffer. You may make another request and so forth.

You need to be aware that for some businesses and many agencies, salary figures are "cast in stone." If you are unsure if this is the case, you may want to ask if the employer has a hard-and-fast salary scale before starting the negotiation. This can spare you from what is an anxiety-evoking part of the interview. Often interviewers will tip you off to this situation with statements such as, "I'm afraid there is very little (or no) flexibility in our salary scale." This does not mean that negotiations should stop. Your next step may be to negotiate additional benefits, such as released time, travel budget, support staff.

Summary

One secret to success in the interview is simple: recognize the intent of the question, reflect on how to best provide the information, and respond by providing the information and by turning requests for negative information into positive information about you if necessary. This is the way to respond to the tough questions that are sure to be a part of any interview.

Another secret is to get your own questions answered. You won't know what to ask if you have not done your homework, however. Lack of homework indicates low motivation or just plain laziness. Why would anyone want to hire you if you don't care enough to do a thorough exploration of the job?

Finally, you need to be prepared to close the deal, if, in fact, the job is offered. Again, if you have done your homework, you will have ideas about what salary is reasonable and what to expect in other aspects of the compensation package. Don't be afraid to haggle if the job is offered. Remember that interviewers become active recruiters once they offer you the job.

Drug Tests, Psychological Inventories, and Physicals

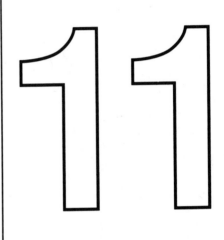

Did you know that drug testing is supported by most employees and that it has generally been upheld by the courts?

There was a time when it was fairly common for companies to subject employees to polygraph tests to determine whether they were honest. In 1989, Congress decided that this type of testing was too intrusive and banned polygraph testing as a means of prescreening or monitoring most employees. The result is that you will not encounter lie detector tests unless you apply for some very specialized law enforcement jobs. However, you will encounter other devices that are designed to determine your physical and mental health, your potential compatibility with other employees, and whether you use illegal drugs. The result: even if you are offered a job, you may have to submit to drug tests, physical examinations, and tests and inventories. Personality inventories and aptitude tests are typically given before an interview and may be a part of the paper file available to the interviewer. In other instances, these instruments are given subsequent to the interview and are used by the personnel department to make final selections.

Regardless of when these devices are administered, you need to be aware of certain facts. First, while you may be indignant about taking drug tests because you are not an illegal substance abuser, they are legal. Moreover, they have been helpful in eliminating potential substance abusers in some industries. Five to eight percent of the 15 million people who were tested last year tested positive, and experts believe that these tests have reduced the incidence of drug use overall, according to Joseph Treaster of the *New York Times.* You may want to ask if you will be subjected to random drug testing on the job so that you can prepare for this eventuality if necessary. My point: you can rail against the unfairness of drug testing if you wish, but it may be interpreted as uncooperative and even suspicious behavior. You will want to ask about the reliability of the testing used by the prospective employer, assert that you are not an illegal substance user, and ask how you can appeal the results in the case of a false positive (your test comes back positive, but you have not used drugs).

Various forms of psychological tests have been used to screen people for jobs since World War I. In more than a few instances, these tests have been abused, and their abuse has resulted in major successful lawsuits against companies such as Duke Power. The result is that companies who use psychological devices must establish that there is a valid relationship between the devices they use and performance on the job in most instances.

While companies may require physical examinations, you cannot be eliminated from employment because of physical handicaps that are unrelated to performance on the job. Effective in 1993, the physical examination must occur after you have been qualified for the job on all other counts. The law was put into place to protect physically handicapped persons from discrimination.

Drug Tests In his 1993 *Knock 'Em Dead* job-seeking manual, Yates suggests that these tests are so unreliable that they are actually a threat to you and your career. I don't doubt some of his assertions about sloppy testing companies and false positive tests because they are well documented. However, there is at least one entire industry that does massive amounts of drug testing without harm to employees because Congress has mandated it: the transportation industry. The employees in that industry do not like the drug-testing program because they feel that the scrutiny is unwarranted. However, I have yet to hear a single story about an employee that was abused by the system. However, there are reliable reports that drug testing in the military has encountered major problems, particularly when it first began in the early eighties. To be sure, there have been some false positives, which is a test that indicates illegal drug usage when none has occurred, and thus some anxious moments for employees. However, there have also been positive tests, and employees who were eliminated could have endangered lives. Consider that 5 percent of all airline employees involved with flights in some capacity tested positive and that drug use is still a leading cause for prospective employee disqualification. Further, 22 percent of the employees connected directly with the safety of train travel for the Amtrak system tested positively.

Illegal substance use is a problem for the modern business, and while the drug-testing system in place is not perfect, there are checks and balances. Should you be worried? Only if you use illegal drugs. You have plenty of recourses if you are abused by the system, including legal action. As noted, at the time a drug test is proposed, ask about your right of appeal in the event you do test positive.

As mentioned, all transportation industries are required by law to give pre-employment drug tests to people who will be directly involved with train, plane, or bus operations. Bus drivers, pilots, dispatchers, air traffic controllers, mechanics, flight attendants, switchers, and others are tested as a result. In these industries, employees are also subjected to random drug testing as well. Federal law enforcement officers are also required to take pre-employment and random drug tests. Other businesses, including nearly half of the Fortune 500 companies, have adopted them as one way to eliminate unreliable employees and reduce health care costs. The Outback Steakhouses and many other not-so-well-known companies have also adopted drug screening programs. Substance abusers have higher absenteeism, are more likely to experience financial problems, may be more inclined toward dishonest activities if they are addicted, and incur higher health costs than nonabusers.

One way that companies screen for illegal drug use is the Bill Clinton test. You may recall that President Clinton was asked during the last presidential campaign if he ever experimented with drugs. His answer was that he tried marijuana, but he didn't inhale, which brought choruses of laughter from a disbelieving public. You may be asked, "Have you ever used illegal drugs?" on an application. Your conscience should be your guide in answering this question. However, the question of greatest concern is whether you are currently using drugs, and thus the reason for drug testing.

The procedure

What does a drug test entail? You are first asked to provide a statement of current medications you are taking, including over-the-counter drugs. This statement is very important, so fill it out completely. Why? Because prescription and nonprescription drugs are the chief cause of false positives, that is, test results that show you are an illicit drug user when in fact you are not. The following is a list of drugs that can result in a false positive test for drug use.

If it is in your system:	You could test positive for:
Ibuprofen (Advil/Nuprin)	Marijuana
Tylenol with Codeine	Heroin
Nytol/Contac/Sudafed	Amphetamines
Valium/Librium	Angel dust
Epinephrine local anesthetic	Heroin
Thorazine	Cocaine
Amoxicillin	Cocaine
Some oriental teas	Marijuana

If you have been taking some or any of these drugs prior to drug testing, you need to know that amphetamines and most barbiturates stay in your system for up to four days. However, secobarbital stays in your system for up to 30 days, as does Valium, Librium, Xanax, Klonopin, and other benzodiazepines. Illegal drugs such as cocaine, PCP, Quaaludes, and other opiates are retained by the body from two to four days. However, chronic users of marijuana and PCP may test positive for 30 days after stopping use of these substances.

Certain foods may also result in false positives. An American Airlines captain tested positive for opium after eating poppy seed rolls that were served on his plane. He was later clear when he was retested. In order to guard against a false positive, you may wish to ask for a list of prescription drugs, nonprescription drugs, and other substances that will result in an inaccurate test. Go over that list and make sure that you note all medicines and foods that you have ingested in the past two or three weeks. If the employer will not provide a list, then note anything that might lead to a false positive test, including pain killers, sleeping aids, all prescription drugs that you take, inhalers and nasal sprays, and sinus or allergy medicines.

After you have completed the form, which will include permission for the company to do the test, you will be asked to provide a urine specimen. You will then be taken to a room, given a container, and then, under minimum supervision, be asked to fill the container. Minimum supervision may mean a person may be in the next room or in the same room with you. You will be provided with privacy in either event. Some companies place a dark blue dye in the commode where the test is being conducted so you will be unable to add water to your specimen. Once you have provided the specimen, its temperature will be checked to see if it is near body temperature to make sure you did not carry it in with you. Typically it will then be divided into samples that will be sealed and sent to a lab for testing.

The urine sample is sent to a drug testing company where it is initially screened, using what is called an Enzyme Multiplied Immunoassay Test, or EMIT for short, which tests for certain substances that indicate the presence of illegal drugs in the urine. If this is positive, a Gas Chromotography test is conducted, which not only confirms the EMIT test but identifies specific drugs that are present in the urine.

How long will drugs stay in the body? It depends on the drug. You will test positive for amphetamines and Darvon if you are tested within 48 hours of usage. Barbiturates may stay in the body up to three weeks, depending on the type, and cocaine and methadone will be present for up to four days, as will opiates such as heroin. Valium will be retained for up to five days, methaqualone up to two weeks, and marijuana five to ten days, depending on usage.

Your worry is, of course, what if you test positive. Some companies have procedures that allow you to be retested if the need arises. Others do not. Prior to leaving the site, you should determine when the results will be returned and whether they will be available to you. You should also determine if retesting is possible. If you are turned down for the job, try to determine if the rejection was due to the drug test.

Faking the test

There is no question that drug tests can sometimes be faked, particularly if you know about them in advance. I have first-hand reports of college athletes that taped urine specimens to the inside of their legs to avoid being detected for steroid use. I have also been told that some employees have diluted samples with water, although this practice is difficult because most companies now use dye in commodes to prevent this from happening. Generally speaking, though, trying to fake these tests is unwise and risky. Not having the drug in your system is the only sure way to avoid a positive test.

Tests and Inventories
Tests

As noted in the introduction, it is not uncommon for companies to ask employees to take tests as a part of the pre-employment screening process. The idea of taking a test can be quite scary for workers who haven't taken tests of any kind for several years. Remember, just because you have been out of school for a while doesn't mean that your brain functioning has slowed or ceased. You think just as well as you ever did.

Tests are devices that measure maximum performance. The intelligence tests and achievement batteries you may have taken in school were designed to measure maximum performance. Many companies use similar devices, called aptitude tests, to measure potential to perform on the job or to complete the training process. While there is no question that tests are better at predicting success in training than on the job, they are used for both purposes.

If you are going to take a test, the best way to prepare for it is to get a good night's sleep, avoid coffee or other beverages or substances with caffeine on the day of the test, and relax. Most people get anxious in these situations, and a cup of coffee can increase nervousness. One cup of coffee can raise your blood pressure and increase your heart rate by 15 beats a minute. You should also wear a watch. The test administrator will keep time, but you will want to keep track of your own progress. If conditions permit, wear comfortable clothing. This is a time to be as relaxed as possible. Finally, if you have a learning disability such as dyslexia or a physical handicap that keeps you from responding as quickly as other people might, ask for special assistance with the test. Companies are obligated to offer this assistance, which will typically involve giving you more time to take the test and providing assistance as needed.

Tests are typically timed and given under very standardized conditions. The test administrator will read the instructions verbatim, ask if you have any questions, and then ask you to open the test booklet and begin. Tests typically use multiple choice formats, that is, you are asked a question and then given four or five possible answers. When you are taking a test you should:

- Make sure you are taking a test, not an inventory. If there is a time limit, you are taking a test of maximum performance.

- Read each question and all possible answers carefully. Then select the answer that seems most correct.

- If you cannot immediately come up with an answer, try to narrow your responses to two that seem like they might fit. Then make your best guess.

- If you cannot narrow the potential answers to two, leave the answer blank and move on. Most tests have what is called a correction-for-guessing formula, and you should never guess blindly. These correction formulas penalize you for wild guessing, and the result is your score is lower than it would have been had you not guessed.

- If you complete the test and you still have some time, go back and review the questions you have not answered. Sometimes you may have picked up a cue to an answer from another question on the test. If you still have more time, review those questions that you have answered. Change only those answers that you know are wrong. Research shows that changing first responses often results in lower test scores.

- If at any time during the taking of a test you find yourself getting nervous to the point that it is impairing your ability to think, put your pencil aside, close your eyes, fill your lungs completely, hold your breath for about five seconds, and then exhale very slowly. Repeat this process about five times, and then return to the test.

Inventories   Inventories, unlike tests, do not measure maximum performance. They measure typical performance. Inventories are used to measure attitudes, personality, values, and interests. Inventories, like tests, must have established validity before they can be used in the screening process, for the most part. The exception to this rule lies in the screening of top-level managers, where inventories are sometimes used indiscriminately, that is, without proper support that they really do produce useful information.

Inventories do not have time limits, so you can proceed at your leisure. If you are interviewing for a top-level management position, you may be given a battery of inventories by a psychologist who will score and interpret the results. In this case, the psychologist is an extension of the interview process and should be treated as such. By this I mean that the research is still for negative information, so answer any questions that arise honestly, but take every opportunity to provide a positive view of yourself and turn positives to negatives.

The instructions for inventories may read as follows: "Read each question and the responses carefully. Then give your first response and move to the next response." You may or may not want to proceed in this fashion, depending on your style. Some people prefer to reflect on the question and consider their answers. Others prefer to work quickly on tasks of this type. Four cautions are in order here. First, inventory results are just as important as test results and should be taken just as seriously. Second, because some inventories are quite long, you can lose your intensity and thus you are not attentive. This can lead to random responses that show up on the lie scales. If you find yourself tiring, get up and walk around and get a drink of water or a cup of coffee. Third, do take time to go back over your inventory. Make sure that you have answered consistently. Fourth, do not spill your coffee on your test if you have made too many changes, as one author suggests. Psychologists are not likely to be fooled by this ploy, and you are providing negative information: you are sloppy in a variety of ways.

There are two schools of thought about taking inventories: one is to try to fake them "good." Krannich suggests that you should never answer these devices honestly and proposes that as you take the inventory you try to imagine what the employer wants, what traits will be required to succeed on the job, and the traits of people who fail. As you are answering the questions, give the winner's answers and avoid the failure's answers. The second school of thought is that you should be honest in your responses. While there is little doubt that in some instances inventories can be faked, there are also some problems, including an ethical one.

Some inventories are quite sophisticated, and it is difficult (although not impossible) to fake them. For example, an inventory may contain a lie scale that is made up of similar items posed in various ways to determine if you are answering consistently. Sometimes lie scales are made up of emotionally laden questions, such as "Have you ever thought about committing suicide?" "Have you ever lied?" "Have you ever stolen anything?" If you answer "no" to any of these questions, you will probably get a point on the lie scale, because almost everyone has thought about what it would be like to commit suicide, has stolen something, or has told a lie.

It is also the case that some inventories used in employee screening appear to have nothing to do with performing the job, but the personnel department has been able to validate its use. In these cases you are stuck. You really have no clues about completing the test questions.

Should you lie? No. There are several reasons for my response. First, unless you are relatively sophisticated, you may in fact disqualify yourself as you try to make yourself look good. Second, it adds more stress to the entire process. Third, and perhaps more importantly, you not only have to get the job, you have to perform the job. The idea that there is no relationship between personnel selection procedures and later performance has often been debated. Some take the view that since the procedures have no validity, it is acceptable to deceive interviewers and lie on tests. The fact is there is considerable support for the use of structured personnel interviews and inventories to select employees. You do not want to get a job in which you will be unsuccessful or unhappy.

Physical Examinations

It is no longer legal for companies to require a prescreening physical examination. However, they may require an interview to establish that you have no physical defects that will keep you from performing the job. They may also want to determine whether you qualify for life insurance, which is a part of many compensation packages. I have already suggested that you have your own physical examination prior to the interview, so the examination itself should pose no problems.

I do want to reiterate that a company cannot refuse to offer you a job on the basis of a physical problem or disability so long as that disability will not prevent you from doing the job.

Summary

For some, drug tests and psychological tests are simply meaningless hoops that must be jumped through on the way to the brass ring: employment. In fact, this process is another opportunity to show that you are a useful and collaborative employee. You will not be hired if you have a bad attitude. However, you do need to be certain that you stand up for your rights during this process as well. No employer will object if you ask about your right to appeal should your drug test result be false positive. Similarly, employers expect people who have learning disabilities or physical handicaps to ask for needed assistance during the testing program. It is your right to be treated fairly during the hiring process. But no employer wants a nuisance, and you will certainly lose any opportunity for employment if there is even a hint of deception. Dishonesty has cost American businesses billions of dollars. The problem of dishonesty has gotten so bad that companies have installed ethics classes. Don't look like a candidate for one of them.

Bad News–Good News: Ending the Search

12

Did you know that more than 5 million people who are not working would work if they could and the main factors that separate those who get jobs and those who don't are job hunting skills and perseverance?

I have tried to be clear about the difficulties of the job search in today's labor market simply because I do not wish to raise any false expectations of easy success. Those types of expectations make the inevitable rejections more difficult to deal with and may cause the job hunter to launch something less than a comprehensive job search effort. This chapter is about dealing with both the bad news and the good news.

Bad News

For every 10 broadcast or hire-me-now-or-in-the-future letters you send, you will get one response. One interpretation of these responses is that you have been rejected nine times. That is a misperception, because many of the employers you contact don't have jobs at the time and don't have the resources needed to write to every job hunter. One business in the North Carolina Research Triangle Park receives 100 unsolicited letters a day. Others receive thousands per year. The message here is to expect no news if you insist on using this strategy, and revel in your success when you get a response.

Getting a response to a broadcast letter has another implication. Eighty to ninety percent of the responses you get will be rejection letters. Get the picture? For each 100 broadcast letters you write, you might get 10 to 20 responses; of those you are going to be successful in getting an interview about one to two percent of the time.

Then there is the question of success in the interview. As you know, it would be a rare employer who would interview only one prospective employee for a job vacancy. More typically an employer might interview from three to five people, depending on the size of the potential employee pool. This means that 66 to 80 percent of all people who interview will get "you-were-great-but-we-hired-someone-else" letters.

If this sounds discouraging, it shouldn't. You simply need to conduct a well-planned, extensive job search in order to be successful.

Learning from Your Rejections

A rejection letter presents an opportunity to learn and increase your job-hunting skills. I suggest that you contact employers who have rejected you on the basis of your cover letter and your resume and ask for feedback about your job-hunting package. Understandably, some employers will be reluctant to provide feedback because of the time that it takes and the fear of legal action. However, if you explain that your only purpose is to improve your resume and cover letter, they may share some honest reactions with you. If they do, be sure to write them a thank-you note.

The same advice stands when you interview: try to get information about your interviewing technique. How well did you present yourself? Did you say inappropriate things? Did you answer questions well? Poorly? Did you get defensive? Did you seem self-confident? You can practice interviewing with a career counselor or coach, but there is no substitute for practicing in the real world. Take any opportunity to find out how you did.

Good News

Once you receive a job offer, complete the salary negotiation, and accept the job, you need to begin to prepare to become a worker again. One of the real advantages you have as a retiree is that working is not new to you. However, just because you have worked doesn't mean that the new job will be a piece of cake. Talking to other employees to find out what to expect on the job can save you from reentry shock, the shock that comes from walking into a new job and finding that things are not as you expected.

You should also carefully review what your job will entail and do an honest assessment of your skills in relationship to the job. It is not unusual to have an "Oh, by the way" clause thrown in at the last minute of the negotiations regarding the job. "Oh, by-the-way, we didn't mention it in the job description, but we just decided that whoever takes this job should be in charge of the dispatch center. How do you feel about that?" "Oh, by the way, we have always used Lotus 1-2-3 spreadsheet programs, but we will be changing to dBase. How do you feel about that?" "Oh, by the way, we are opening a plant in Mexico, and we noticed that you speak a little Spanish. How do you feel about going to Mexico once a month to represent the parent company?" Obviously you have the right to add your own "Oh, by the way, I don't want to do that," which opens up a variety of potential problems, not the least of which is you won't get the job. The other option is to learn about dispatch, enroll in a dBase course, or brush up on your Spanish.

Multiple Good News

Every job hunter wants to pick and choose from the best of the available jobs. Multiple job offers allow you to be selective to some degree. They may also allow you more leverage in negotiating salary, fringe benefits, and perks. If you get one job offer that meets your needs, congratulate your-self. If you get multiple offers, celebrate.

Summary   It is a truism in most job hunts that you will get more bad news than good news. However, one bit of good news more than makes up for lots of bad news. Take the bad news in stride, and enjoy the good news.

Volunteering

13

Did you know there are 175,000 volunteer organizations in the United States?

Opportunities for volunteering abound in our society, and except for the fact that volunteers are unpaid, the challenges and rewards are just as great as they are in the regular work world. There are many ways to become a volunteer, and some of the more interesting ones will be explored in this chapter.

The Mentality of the Volunteer

If you have spent all your life pursuing extrinsic rewards (translate that to money), volunteering may be difficult. Why? Because to be a good volunteer, your source of reward will have to be intrinsic. Oh sure, people will be appreciative of your efforts, and they will say so. But just as it is in the work-for-pay world, volunteers find themselves performing many thankless tasks. Taking tickets at a museum, working in the gift shop at the local hospital, registering people who volunteer to give blood, and tutoring a recalcitrant fourth grader are all worthwhile activities, but they may not be highly rewarding in the sense that you may not see wonderful things happen as a result of your work. Since you will not be paid, the results may be less than satisfactory, or, to put it differently, you may be less than satisfied. Elwood Chapman, in the second edition of his best-selling retirement planning book *Comfort Zones,* suggests that there are many possible rewards that may result from volunteering, including giving something back. These rewards are comradeship, recognition for your achievements as a volunteer, a sense of mission, an active mind, a chance to develop new skills, a substitute for out-and-out leisure, the chance to work with compatible people, and the freedom to withdraw whenever you like. Earlier in the book, I noted that volunteers have greater flexibility than employed workers because they set their own hours. The point is that you need to find a volunteer activity that will allow you to feel good about what you are doing, or you will lose your motivation.

In order to increase the likelihood that you will feel good about your volunteer efforts, engage in only those activities that are of interest. Make sure that you really want to participate, and avoid volunteering because you feel now that you are retired you ought to try to "give a little back."

National Volunteer Organizations

As was noted in the question introducing this chapter, there are numerous organizations that sponsor volunteer activities. We will look at a few of these national organizations here. Although these are national organizations, each one has local chapters. Generally speaking, you can check your local telephone book to get the number of the local chapter. You can also call the national organization for the chapter nearest you.

Retired Senior Volunteer Program (RSVP)

This organization is a part of ACTION, the Federal Domestic Volunteer Agency. ACTION sponsors other volunteer programs including the Foster Grandparent Program, the Senior Companion Program, and the Student Community Service Program. Currently RSVP involves more than 500,000 volunteers working in 51,000 communities. The headquarters for RSVP is located at 806 Connecticut Avenue, Washington, D.C. 20525. RSVP provides volunteer options for people over 60 who are retired or semiretired. Local chapters offer opportunities for tutoring young people, enhancing adult literacy, assisting the chronically ill, helping teenage parents, fighting drug and alcohol abuse, and a variety of others. The organization asks you to fill out a registration card so they can match your skills to the needs of the communities. They also offer an insurance program that protects you from any liability that results from your volunteer work.

National Executive Service Corp (NESC)

NESC is headquartered at 257 Park Avenue South, New York, New York 10010. This organization has 34 local chapters located primarily in urban areas throughout the United States. The objective of NESC is to assist nonprofit organizations by providing consulting services through a cadre of volunteer consultants who, for the most part, are retired corporate executives.

Service Corporation of Retired Executives (SCORE)

This organization is located at 1825 Connecticut Avenue, NW, Suite 503, Washington, D.C. 20009. SCORE is sponsored by the Small Business Administration and has as its primary objective helping people who operate small businesses. This is accomplished by recruiting former business executives who consult with small business owners. Currently, over 12,000 retirees volunteer their services through SCORE.

National Association of Partners in Education (NAPE)

NAPE is located at 119 South Asaph Street, Alexandria, Virginia 22314. Its function is to encourage people who like children to get involved in the educational process through volunteering. NAPE has numerous local chapters that function in conjunction with local school districts. If you are interested in becoming an educational volunteer, contact the administrative offices of your local school district.

American Association of Retired People (AARP)

AARP is located at 3200 East Carson Street, Lakewood, California 90712. It operates a Volunteer Talent Bank of 9,000 people who want to volunteer. AARP matches the volunteers to their own needs as well as to those of other organizations, such as the National Park Service.

AARP's 4,000 local chapters are also extensively involved in volunteerism in their communities. If you have not joined AARP already, you can do so by sending $8.00 to AARP, POB 199, Long Beach, California 90801. When you join AARP, you have the option of joining one of its divisions, the National Retired Teachers Association, if you have worked in the field of education.

The National Red Cross

The National Red Cross is headquartered in Washington, D.C., but to become a volunteer, you must contact your local Red Cross chapter. Since there are over 2,800 chapters nationwide, you should have no problem finding one in your area, although I found that some of the local chapters list themselves geographically (e.g., Orange County Red Cross), which makes them harder to find in the telephone book. However, the National Red Cross can assist you if you are unable to find the listing for your chapter.

The Red Cross operates a training program for its volunteers. These training programs tend to be job specific, so it is important for you to understand what may be of interest to you. After you are properly trained, you may be able to assist in a variety of tasks, ranging from organizing a blood donor drive to assisting with disaster relief. Incidentally, volunteering to assist people who have been victimized by natural disasters such as earthquakes may take you away from home for two weeks or more.

National Retiree Volunteer Center (NRVC)

NRVC is located at 607 Marquette Avenue, Minneapolis, MN 55402. This agency works with business and industry to help its employees establish volunteer agencies. If you have not yet retired, you may wish to determine if your company has an NRVC-sponsored retirement group already established.

Service clubs

Lions clubs, Kiwanis clubs, Jaycees, the Shrine, Rotarians, and other service clubs have thousands of local chapters dedicated to improving eyesight and helping the blind, providing money to support children's hospitals, and a myriad of other worthwhile services. The presidents or membership chairs of your local club will be glad to give you more details about the goals of their organization and how you can become involved.

State and Local Opportunities for Volunteerism

There are probably hundreds of organizations that sponsor volunteers at the national level. There are tens of thousands of state and local organizations that have the same aim, that is, to provide services to people by providing volunteers. We will look at a few of these here.

Political parties

Ever dream of running for public office or reforming local government? You can act on this dream by getting involved with your favorite political party at the local or state level. Typically the state organization is headquartered in your state's capitol and your local organization in your city or county (or both). If you cannot locate them, simply call an elected official of your party, and he or she will tell you how you can join the ranks.

Getting involved in politics doesn't have to mean partisanship. It can mean dealing with issues instead of candidates. Has one of your favorite bond issues failed to pass? Get involved and try to change the outcome the next time. Taxes too high? Join the ranks of the local taxpayers' association and try to get the tax levy reduced. Think schools need to be improved? Join or form a group that will sponsor school board candidates that will make a difference. Better yet, run yourself. Serving as an elected official is a great form of volunteerism.

Churches

More people volunteer their services to and through churches than any other institution. Churches sponsor a variety of activities, ranging from feeding the homeless to missionary work. They also need countless volunteers to teach church school and to serve on boards and commissions if they are going to function properly. Talk to your priest, minister, or rabbi about the opportunities in your church.

Schools

Private and public schools depend upon volunteers for tutoring services, to work as teacher's aides, to monitor bus stops and school crossings, and to assist with activities such as plays and concerts. Call the administrative offices of your local school district, and it is likely that you will find a volunteer coordinator who has many interesting things for you to do.

Hospitals

As hospital costs have risen, hospital administrators have turned to volunteers to run information desks, operate the gift shop, answer telephones on the ward, provide clerical services, deliver mail and flowers to rooms, read to patients, lead support groups, and manage a variety of other services. This emphasis on volunteerism will increase in the future.

Law enforcement

Many police forces have formed teams of volunteers to escort women at night as a rape prevention effort, provide transportation to people who have had too much to drink, and to work as part of a team to patrol high crime areas.

Volunteer fire departments

It is not unusual for suburban and rural areas to have volunteer fire departments. Members of these departments have regular meetings, periodic training sessions, and drills. If you are looking for a volunteer position that is of vital importance to the community in which you live, this is it.

Paramedics and emergency services

Paramedics must undergo training ranging from routine first aid to delivering babies, and in many communities, they are paid for their services. However, there are still many communities that depend upon volunteers to provide emergency services to people injured in accidents or who develop other types of medical emergencies.

Hospices and nursing homes

Hospices and nursing homes are often understaffed and need the services of volunteers to perform services ranging from reading to people to fund raising.

Cultural organizations

Your local symphony, local theater, art museum, and other cultural groups need your services. Fund raising, building sets, marketing tickets, taking tickets at performances, acting as extras, performing, and supervising outings for children are a few of the services that you might perform. The arts as we know them would not exist without the services of thousands of volunteers.

Meals on Wheels   These community-based programs deliver hot meals to the homebound. Your job as a volunteer is to pick up and deliver the meals.

Veteran's organizations   If you are a veteran, you have the option of becoming involved with several organizations, including the Veterans of Foreign Wars and the American Legion. These organizations offer a variety of opportunities to become involved in volunteer activities that relate both to veterans and to broader communities.

Recreational organizations   Most cities and towns run recreation leagues for children and adults. These leagues need coaches, referees, umpires, score keepers, and other workers to assist with the teams. In some instances, some of these workers are paid a small fee for their services, but typically they are unpaid volunteers. If you are interested in intramural sports, call your local recreation department to local activities.

Big brother/sister organizations and foster grandparents   Because of the high divorce rate and the mobility of the American family, many children are left with too little support from their families. You can help with this nationwide problem by becoming a big brother or sister or a foster grandparent. The Department of Social Services, typically a part of your county government, can help you locate these organizations.

Summary   There are hundreds of thousands of volunteers filling a wide variety of jobs ranging from business consultant to baby sitter. Their work is very significant, and because of the unmet needs in our society, more volunteers are in demand than ever before. If you do decide to volunteer, you need to engage in an activity that will meet your needs while you are helping others meet theirs. If you do not concern yourself about your own needs, you are likely to be as unhappy as the paid worker who is in an unsatisfactory job, but you will not have the benefit of a paycheck to keep you motivated.

Looking Ahead

Research tells us that successful workers of all ages are futurists.

Become a Futurist

A friend of mine who claims to be a futurist was asked how a person becomes a futurist. His answer: "By deciding to be one." What he means is that futurists decide that it is important to them to anticipate future happenings and then begin to attend to things that will help them predict what is going to occur. Many "retired" workers were caught not looking at the future, or they would have anticipated that their companies would change and their jobs would be in jeopardy. Ten years ago, every major newspaper in the country carried the story that it cost General

Motors over one thousand dollars more to manufacture a car than it did Ford or Chrysler. The implication was that GM had to reduce costs to stay competitive. The outcome was thousands of workers lost their jobs as GM went on a cost-cutting binge.

Every day, newspapers, magazines, and television shows produce information that tells us about the future. We all know that we are going to see a remarkable change in the way health care is delivered. Why? Because people can no longer afford the current system. How will it change? What jobs will be effected? Again, that information is delivered to us every day. I'm not suggesting that you track all the trends that influence our society, only that you track the trends that influence you and your career.

Embarking on a retirement career means embracing new challenges. Starting a new career requires us to look forward, not backward. To focus on the past is to accept the stereotype of what it is like to grow older and retire. Employers want vital, forward-looking people, because success in business depends upon the employee's ability to anticipate the trends that shape our society and to act in ways that will take advantage of those trends. Successful workers of the future will relish change and see it as an opportunity. Just as they will anticipate changes in our society, they will identify their own need for change and act. If you long for the "good old days," you are spending too much time in the past.

I am not suggesting that you should reject the past, only that you not live in the past. Retirees must continue to look ahead, to anticipate those changes that will influence their lives and their careers. The constant in the future will be change, change that will occur with increasing rapidity. You have two choices at this juncture in your life: be an observer or a player. In the section that follows, some of the trends that will shape your life and your career are discussed. If you are not already a futurist, begin now to predict how these trends will influence your life and career.

Trends to the Year 2000 and Beyond

The global economy will create new, undreamed-of career opportunities. The North American Free Trade Agreement (NAFTA), which created a free trade zone with Mexico and Canada, was hotly debated, with the likelihood that the points made by both sides were correct. The United States will lose some of its low-paying jobs to Mexico. New markets will be opened that will lead to new jobs in this country. But the most exciting possibilities lie in the area of creating new business arrangements among financial institutions, manufacturers, health-care providers, the media, and other businesses. We do not know how these changes will occur, but I can assure you that the people who figure out the answers to the questions will be the successful people of tomorrow.

NAFTA is just the beginning. We see fledgling businesses starting in the former Soviet Union with the aid of foreign capital. Entrepreneurs are starting a new airline to compete with Aeroflot. There are opportunities for small businesses as well as for people who simply want to go abroad and work. At this time there is a desperate need for an employment placement group to recruit and place American workers in foreign countries. Someone will fill that void, perhaps before this book is printed, because that is how rapidly developments occur.

Women, minorities, and older workers will make up an increasing share of the labor force. If you return to work or start your own business, you will find that your colleagues and employees will increasingly be women and minorities. These two groups will make up the bulk of the labor pool. Sexism and racism will continue in our society, but there will be less tolerance of racists and sexists in the workplace.

The young woman of today will spend, on average, half of her life working, which is approximately 39 years. Older women, like older men, will enter or return to paying jobs, but often not for the same reasons. They will return to ease the boredom of the empty nest, escape their newly retired husbands, fill the void left by the death of spouses, and, of course, to make money to make up for the inadequacies of pension plans and Social Security.

Because of shortages of skilled workers in some occupations, increased longevity, and better health care, older workers are staying in their jobs longer or turning to new careers. Antidiscrimination laws will also help fuel this trend, but the biggest factor will be the increased realization that older workers contribute knowledge, skills, and stability not found in younger workers. The bottom line here is that if you stay in the labor force or return to it, you will be joining many others who have decided that working is the best retirement option for them.

Small businesses will continue to be the greatest source of new jobs in our labor market. Earlier I discussed the entire matter of starting your own business and provided some guidelines for doing so. Entrepreneurs with businesses with fewer than 100 employees will continue to fuel the job growth in our society. The rewards of starting some of these new businesses will be high, but so are the risks in some cases. It has been said that these businesses simultaneously offer the best chances of making you rich and broke. Even if you do not wish to start your own business, you may want to focus your job search on newly emerging businesses.

Nontraditional career selection will accelerate. Selecting a nontraditional career means entering an occupation dominated by the opposite gender, that is, an occupation that is made up by over 70 percent of the opposite sex. Women have made the first move and are now streaming into areas that were once bastions of masculinity. However, men will not be able to continue to ignore the opportunities that abound in health care and other fields where women have dominated. When I suggested that he consider nursing, a young Hispanic client bristled at the idea. At first he thought I was casting aspersions at his manhood. However, as we looked further at salary ($35,000 in his area), job security (excellent), fringe benefits (health and dental insurance fully paid), working conditions (has the option of working from Friday afternoon until Monday morning for a full week's pay), and the opportunity to meet dozens of young women, he began to consider nursing as a viable option. Older workers who are embarking on new careers should give serious consideration to nontraditional occupations in health care and elsewhere. In the long run there will be no nontraditional careers, only careers.

Technology, particularly computer technology, will reshape the workplace. There is a raging debate among academics about whether workers of tomorrow will need to understand how to use computers. Some argue that we will make our computers dumber, and therefore we do not have to make our workers smarter. What is meant by this is that to some degree we have the capacity to program machines such as computers so that they can "tell" us how to operate them, and therefore workers of the future will not need to know about them.

While the academic debate goes on, the Bureau of Labor Statistics projects that computer systems analysts and computer programmers will be two of the fastest-growing occupations in our country. Perhaps more importantly, many workers, ranging from auto mechanics and financial analysts to architects and engineers, find that, in order to do their jobs, they must understand how to deal with computers. One of my cars has several computer chips that regulates various functions in the car. A friend's house has an alarm system, lighting system, heating system, and entertainment system that are all regulated by a computer. Many of my colleagues get messages on E-Mail, which is an electronic mail system that allows people all over the country to communicate using modems and computers. Another friend logs on to Prodigy and one or two other systems to manage his own portfolio.

We may be able to make computers dumber, but it is also clear that everyone who works will need to be far more than computer literate. If you are returning to the labor market, begin by upgrading your computer skills to the point where you can do word processing and basic work with spreadsheet programs. Then find out what other skills are needed in the field you intend to enter. Just as importantly, keep up with the technology of computers. I bought the computer I prepared this manuscript on three years ago. I called about getting the memory increased so I could add another software package, only to be told that it is an old computer. It is true. Our technology becomes obsolete every three years.

Guess what? The most exciting part is yet to come. You have undoubtedly heard of the information highway that will be delivered to our living rooms via cable television and telephone lines. Yes, we will be able to access hundreds of channels on our television sets, but that doesn't mean that we will have four championship wrestling programs instead of two. It does mean that we will have endless opportunities to buy things, invest our money, improve our skills, earn basic and advanced degrees, learn a foreign language, watch plays in New York and Los Angeles, and tune in to English soccer matches in Manchester.

Also accessing dozens of data banks, including entire libraries and information brokers, will become common. Perhaps even better, we will be able to acquire a college education without leaving home if we choose to upgrade our computer literacy skills. We will be able to take bridge lessons and get a few golf tips without having to suffer through a commercial for a golf magazine.

Much of our job training and retraining will occur at home. Just as importantly, more and more people will never leave home to go to work. They will use their computer at home to perform a variety of tasks, ranging from booking airlines reservations (already happens) to tutoring youngsters in algebra.

Changes in the manufacturing sector and increases in the service sector of our economy will make communications skills a prerequisite for success in most jobs. We have all been made aware that there has been a relative reduction in manufacturing jobs in our economy and a relative and real increase in service jobs such as personal service, health care, education, and recreation. This trend will continue unabated.

What may have escaped our attention is that the changes that have occurred have placed a premium on the ability to communicate and relate to others. Automobiles are manufactured on platforms by teams that constantly interact to improve quality and productivity. Health care involves a team approach that includes physicians, nurses, technologists, and therapists. Without adequate communication, both our cars and our bodies will deteriorate. Many of our businesses require good customer relations skills, including retail sales, financial services, legal services, and public relations. The need for good human relationship skills is so profound that the U.S. Department of Labor lists it as a basic skill, just as mathematical and verbal skills are essential to success in most occupations.

You can improve your communication skills in a wide variety of ways, the easiest of which is to read some of the excellent books on human relationships. If you are starting your own business, developing good communications skills is critical if you hope to be successful.

Jobs will increasingly call for workers to be better educated. Students graduate from high school today with language and mathematical skills that are substantially below those needed to perform many of the new jobs being created. As an older worker, your language and mathematical skills may be substandard as well. Fortunately, community colleges and vocational technical schools offer the courses you need to upgrade your skills to the highest levels. Earlier I made the pitch that middle-aged and older workers learn just as well as adolescents and young adults. Our belief that we do not stems from our acceptance of several myths about older people. If you truly want a second career, as opposed to a job, you need to get an accurate assessment of your own skill level and get started.

Summary   Successful workers keep one watchful eye on the future and the other eye the present. Retired workers can enhance their credibility in the workplace by doing the same thing. They may long for the past, but they know that it will not return, and the best thing to derive from the past is lessons for the present and future. Become a futurist by beginning to think and project how today's happenings will influence tomorrow's events.

APPENDIX A: Electronic Record Data Base Directory

America Online Distribution Center
Suite 200
8619 Westwood Center Drive
Vienna, VA 22182

Offers many data bases, including Career Center, which includes job listings and a resume-writing program. Fees: 10-hour free trial offer available. Monthly membership fee of $9.95, which includes five free hours on line per month. After five hours, fee is $3.95 per hour.

BRS Information Technology
8000 West Park Drive
McLean, VA 22101

Has a Corptech directory that can be used to search for technical and engineering positions. Fees: $106 per hour to search Corptech.

Datatimes, Inc.
Parkway Plaza, Suite 450
1400 Quail Springs Parkway
Oklahoma City, OK 73134

Career file includes *Talent for Hire,* which is a job seeker's guide and a *Career Enhancement Guide* for new executives. Fees: $85 start-up fee, plus charges for each page of information accessed.

Dun's Electronic Business Directory
Three Sylvan Way
Parsippany, NJ 07054

Services include job searches by job type, company, and region. Business career only. Part of Dialog Information Services. Fees: $295 start-up plus $1.20 per minute of use. Also a printing cost of .30–.50 per record.

G.E. Information Services
Client Services
401 North Washington Street
Rockville, MD 20850

"Dr. Job" File includes a question-and-answer column with career and employment experts. Fees: Monthly fee of $8.95 for four hours. Three dollars per hour when the minimum is exceeded except during peak hours (6:00 to 8:00 P.M.), which costs $12.50 per hour.

Human Resources Information Network
Executive Telecom System International
College Park North
9585 Valparaiso Court
Indianapolis, IN 46268

Job Ads data base represents one of 100 data bases. Primarily for use by companies, not individuals. Fees: Variable, depending on data base selected.

Job Bank USA
1420 Spring Hill Road
McLean, VA 22101

Services include a resume bank.

Electronic networking: Allows people to connect with unlisted job openings. Considered most active job data bank by some experts.

Career tool kit: Receive quarterly newsletter about market techniques and a catalog of services. Members get discounts on various services in catalog.

Career fitness: Exercises to build a healthier career.

Toll-free access: Get feedback from staff/career counselor about how to improve resume.

Service scans resume completely into data base.

When job openings and applicants are matched, applicants are called for a prescreening (Are they still interested? Do they need to make any updates to resume?) and upon their release resumes are given to employer.

Fee: Individuals, $75 per year; $48.50 per year through affinity groups such as alumni association. Employers, $250 per search (less for multiple searches).

NEWSNET, INC.
945 Haverford Road
Bryn Mawr, PA 19010

Provides Dunn and Bradstreet and TRW reports on a variety of companies. No career data base, but useful information when researching companies. Fees: $15 per month; $120 per month plus on-line fee.

The New York Times FASTRAK
P.O. Box 3066
Chicago, Illinois 60654

Creates an electronic version of your resume that is made available to FASTRAK employers within minutes. Participants can call as often as they want and send resumes to up to five employers per call. Participants use classified employment ads in *New York Times* and call in the code for the participating employers. Fee: $40 gives you six months of unlimited use.

Prodigy Services Company
445 Hamilton Avenue
White Plains, NY 10601

Careers bulletin board: members post job listings or jobs-wanted notices, which are broken down into areas. Contains job-hunting advice. Fees: $14.95 per month for two hours' usage.

Standard and Poor's On-Line Services
Standard and Poor's Corporation
25 Broadway
New York, NY 10004

Executive data base: Biographical data bases of 70,000 executives for networking purposes. Gives information about schools they attended, their degrees, and the company they are working for. Corporate data bases: Directory of 55,000 corporations, both public and private. Gives financial information about companies, CEO information, contact person. Most companies listed are in the United States, some are outside the United States. Fee: Go through dialog; $84 per on-line hour, $2 per record of information.

Technical Employment News Job Listings
12416 Haymeadow Drive
Austin, TX 78750

Technical careers only. Produces weekly publication regarding careers throughout the United States and abroad. Fees: $55 for 52 issues per year. Also includes annual directory of technical firms.

APPENDIX B: References

Baxter, Neale. "Resumes, Application Forms, Cover Letters, and Interviews." *Occupational Outlook Quarterly,* Spring 1987.

Beatty, Richard. *175 High-Impact Cover Letters.* New York: Wiley, 1992.

Brown, Duane, and Carol W. Minor. *Career Needs in a Diverse Workforce.* Alexandria, VA.: NCDA, 1992.

Case, John. "How to Succeed without a Job." *Inc.,* June 1992.

Chapman, Elwood. *Comfort Zones: Planning Your Future.* Los Altos, Calif.: Crisp, 1990.

Eder, Robert W. and Gerald Ferris. *The Job Interview.* Beverly Hills: Sage, 1989.

Eliason, Carol. *The Business Plan for the Homebased Business.* Washington, D.C.: U.S. SBA.

Editors of *Entrepreneur* magazine. *184 Businesses That Anyone Can Start and Make a Lot of Money.* 2d ed. New York: Bantam Books, 1990.

Evaluating Franchise Opportunities. Washington, D.C.: SBA.

Eyler, D. R. *Starting and Managing a Business from Your Home.* New York: John Wiley, 1992.

Gumpert, David E. *How to Really Start Your Own Business.* Boston: Inc Publishing, 1991.

"Human Capital: The Decline of America's Workforce." *BusinessWeek,* (September 1988): 100–119.

Editors of *Income* magazine. *33 Profitable Part-Time Businesses.* New York: Prentice Hall, 1992.

Kahn, Sharon and the Philip Lief Group. *101 Best Businesses to Start.* New York: Doubleday, 1992.

Kramer, Farrell. "Path to a Nation of Consultants." Associated Press, September 1993.

Krannich, Carol Rae and L. Robert. *Dynamite Answers to Interview Questions: No More Sweaty Palms.* Woodbridge, Va.: Impact, 1992.

Lewis, Robert. "For Whom the Job Bell Doesn't Toll." *Bulletin 35,* no. 2, 1994.

———. "Networking, New Tactics Lift Older Job Seekers." *Bulletin 34,* no. 2, 1993.

Marsh, Deloss L. *Retirement Careers.* Charlotte, Vt.: Williamson Publishing, 1991.

McDaniels, Carl. *The Changing Workplace.* San Francisco: Jossey-Bass, 1989.

McDermott, Michael J., ed. *Business Opportunities Handbook.* Milwaukee: Enterprise Magazines, 1992.

Michelozzl, Betty Neville. *Coming Alive from Nine to Five: The Career Search Handbook.* 4th ed. Mountainview, Calif.: Mayfield Publishing Co., 1992.

Petras, Kathryn and Ross. *The Over-40 Job Guide.* New York: Poseidon, 1993.

Porter, Sylvia. *Planning Your Retirement.* New York: Prentice Hall, 1991.

Powell, C. Randolph. *Career Planning.* 2d ed. Dubuque: Kendall/Hunt, 1990.

Robinson, David. *What Is an Entrepreneur?* Holbrook, Mass.: Bob Jones, 1990.

Satterfield, Mark. *Where the Jobs Are.* Hawthorne, N.J.: Careers Press, 1992.

Savageau, David. *Retirement Places Rated.* New York: Prentice Hall, 1990.

Sinetar, Marsha. *Do What You Love and the Money Will Follow.* New York: Dell, 1987.

Stern, Linda. "How to Find a Job." *Modern Maturity* (February–March 1993): 25–30; 32–34.

Sukiennik, Diane, Lisa Raufman, and William Bendat. *The Career Fitness Program.* 3d ed. Scottsdale: Gorsuch Scarisbrick, 1992.

Treaster, Joseph B. "Drug Testing Gains Favor among Firms throughout the Country," New York: New York Times News Service, 1993.

U.S. Department of Labor. *Career Guide to Industries.* Washington, D.C.: U.S. Government Superintendent of Documents, 1992.

————. *Occupational Outlook Handbook.* Washington, D.C.: U.S. Government Printing Office, 1992–93.

————. *Occupational Projections and Training Data.* Washington, D.C.: U.S. Government Printing Office, 1992.

U.S. Department of Labor. *Tips for Finding the Right Job.* Washington, D.C.: U.S. Superintendent of Documents, 1991.

Yates, M. *Knock 'Em Dead: The Ultimate Job Seekers Book.* Holbrook, Mass.: Bob Adams, 1993.

Waymon, Lynn. *Starting and Managing Your Own Business from Your Home.* Washington, D.C.: U.S. Government Printing Office, 1986.

VGM CAREER BOOKS

 VGM Career Horizons
a division of *NTC Publishing Group*
4255 West Touhy Avenue
Lincolnwood, Illinois 60646–1975